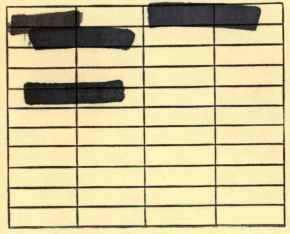
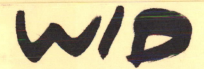

ACHILLES' CHOICE

Achilles' Choice

Examples of Modern Tragedy

David Lenson

Princeton University Press *1975*

Library of Congress Cataloging in Publication Data will
be found on the last printed page of this book

Publication of this book has been aided by a grant
from the Andrew W. Mellon Foundation

This book has been composed in Linotype Janson

Printed in the United States of America
by Princeton University Press, Princeton, New Jersey

for June Lenson

Prefatory Note

This study is undertaken as an act of speculative criticism, not as an act of scholarship, not as an act of literary history. I mean this to be a flat statement of fact, neither a boast nor an apology. Criticism of tragedy is an over-populated field. It has advanced beyond the stage of groundwork, perhaps even beyond maturation. It requires, just as all developed areas of criticism require, a sense of exploration that neither ignores the precedent traditions, nor allows them to tyrannize. Works of speculation at their best have given scholars new stimuli; at their worst they have been forgotten with no harm done. It is only because the public for such works is limited to specialists that it is necessary to issue the following disclaimers.

I have tried to avoid deriving a definition of tragedy. In the period during which this book was written, the marriage of philosophy and linguistics has encouraged in criticism, as in, for example, the social sciences, a hunger for terminology. The prospect of devoting further effort to these matters seems barren. The precise, useful, but ultimately reductive work of Oscar Mandel ought to remain the crowning effort of this kind in the field of tragedy. Definition, by definition, as it were, signals an erection of boundaries. Where such boundaries exist, a given point must lie on one side or the other. I have never found it illuminating to answer a flat "yes" or "no" to the question of whether or not such-and-such a work is a tragedy. It is more helpful in the final analysis to think of tragic elements or "norms"—to borrow Wellek's term—which a given work may contain in greater or lesser density. The result of this attitude is a flexible, fairly liberal idea of a tradition. This proves a telling advantage in the interpretation of more recent events.

On the other hand, an historical survey or "history of tragedy" during the modern epoch, done well, would be a collection of potential topics for research, or, done poorly, a blur of name-dropping. Such works exist, and there is no need for another. My more or less chronological arrangements of topics may seem to promise some species of diced-up history, a kind of linear *gestalt*. All that is meant is a choice of certain essential moments in the formation of the modern tragic tradition. Of necessity, these selections must be viewed as examples. Examples point past themselves to a larger set, yet it is wrong, in my opinion, thereby to preclude interest in an example for its own sake. Admittedly, the points which make a particular work interesting to a student of tragedy may not be the same as those which award the work its place in general literary history. It is to be stressed that if I have given Kleist more space than Goethe this does not mean that I am making a heretical judgment about the comparative overall significance of the two.

The books, friends, and teachers who have contributed to my thinking on this subject are too numerous to mention. I have had the opportunity to listen to classes and lectures by some of the leading critics in this field, notably Francis Fergusson, Walter Kaufmann and George Steiner, and I gleaned great benefit from them all. But my primary debt is to the Program in Comparative Literature of Princeton University, in particular its chairman, Professor Robert Fagles, whose guidance and expenditure of time extended long past the dissertational days of this project. It is customary at times such as these to grant a teacher the credit for what follows, while the author accepts the blame. So extensively have I looted this most impressive thinker, however, that I am tempted to assign him some of the blame as well.

Table of Contents

ACHILLES' CHOICE

1 *Paradoxes of Tragedy*

> For my mother Thetis the goddess of the silver feet tells
> me / I carry two sorts of destiny toward the day of my
> death. Either, / if I stay here and fight beside the city of
> the Trojans, / my return home is gone, but my glory
> shall be everlasting; / but if I return home to the beloved
> land of my fathers, / the excellence of my glory is gone,
> but there will be a long life / left for me, and my end in
> death will not come to me quickly.
>
> (*Iliad*, trans. Lattimore, IX, 410f.)

Achilles' choice is the archetype of the decision faced by
every tragic hero. In the City Dionysia of Athens it is
built into the very construction of the theatre. Down
below, the chorus performs its odes and dances, collective
and nameless, while above them on the stage declaim the
masks of ancient heroes, unending names. The heroes act;
the song re-acts to them, just as long ago the ancestors of
those singers might have passed from lip to lip a recent
rumor from Troy. The polarity is expressed in every possible way: spatially, linguistically, ethically, religiously,
temporally. Every unified vision of life is shattered.

Greek culture is always prone to the universal, not the
unified. The only way to express the fullness of existence is to articulate the extremes, and this is what they
do. Every member of the audience feels the dichotomy
personally. Greece is, after all, at once the self-proclaimed, self-contained zenith of civilization, and at the
same time a trading, exploring, colonizing power at arms.

Accordingly, a man could be a farmer, living anonymously close to the seasons and the land, or he could be a soldier, seeking in the emptiness between small outposts a dream of glory, and a name. It is, in short, the dialectic between Ithaka and Ilion, between the *Odyssey* with its centripetal motion towards love and home, and the *Iliad* with its centrifugal reach into Asia Minor, into wrath. The *Iliad* is full of names. But Greece and Greek tragedy are the sum of both.

This kind of cultural immediacy seems distant to us now when we think of tragedy. Overheard on the street or from a radio, the word evokes the reaction, "Who died?" rather than, "In which theatre?" Only the very old or very evil escape it in their eulogies. It maintains a sense of sudden or undeserved catastrophe, or particularly public misfortune. Its association with a feeling of necessity makes it useful for relieving the living of their guilt and responsibility. Yet for all this if a writer chooses to label a literary work a tragedy, he still encounters an active convention against which his work will be judged in one way or another. Somehow a set of critical norms defines a tradition. The educated man who sneers at the common use of the word must have some more elevated notion in mind, yet if pressed on the matter he will probably be at a loss. In truth there is no coherent definition or even description of tragic art which has any wide subscription today. There is no single indispensable work on the subject, and no one writer who is universally acknowledged as the rightful heir of the tradition.

The two norms most often agreed upon are, unfortunately, useless and misleading. The first of these is generic, the assertion that tragedy is a type of drama.

This thesis arose, not surprisingly, during those periods when tragedy *was* indeed flourishing on the stage. When it was not, during the Middle Ages for example, it was envisioned as a pattern of action, in Chaucer a kind of recapitulation of Boethian Fortune with its rise and fall. So too in the twentieth century, when drama is not the central genre, tragedy is frequently considered a philosophical system, or "sub-philosophy," as Unamuno calls it. In addition, we have lived through a century and a half during which the impulse to tragedy exceeded the dramaturgical skills of the best authors. Byron, Shelley, Browning, Mallarmé, and James were failed playwrights who came, in time, to apply their understanding of tragic action to genres in which they were more talented. Novels and even lyric poems were written that attempted to recreate certain elements of Greek and Shakespearean plays.

It is a general rule that from the beginning tragedy tended to gravitate toward the literary and social centers of the times. It was so long allied with drama mainly because drama was the genre that satisfied this need. More practical factors, such as the desire of authors for economic survival, certainly enter into the picture. It should not be surprising to observe that tragedy followed the changes in generic predominance that took place during the eighteenth century, when drama was on the decline and the lyric and novel in the ascendant. To neglect the application of centuries of criticism simply to protect a preconceived idea of genre is clearly wrong, particularly since that critical strain has long been part of the mainstream of literary thought. Furthermore, there has been, as I hope to show, a particularly productive interchange between critics and practitioners during the last hundred and fifty years, and this interchange is not nullified by the fact that the critics were usually writing about the drama while the practitioners were engaged in other genres.

This false generic norm has long impeded wide understanding of the nature of tragedy. But it is overshadowed by the second false norm, one which involves much more complex and difficult issues. This is the idea that tragedy must have an unhappy ending, and that closing disaster is the earmark of the tradition. The *Oresteia* ought to have shattered this notion from the very start, yet it persists largely because of Shakespeare, Racine, and their successors, with their terminal bloodbaths. But consider the *Oresteia*. It shares with catastrophic tragedies a fundamental sense of extremes, a collision of forces which, as Hegel indicated, are as right as they are contradictory. In the clash of right and right, there are only two possibilities: either one or both of the forces will be destroyed, or else the world must be substantially altered to comprehend both. The *Oresteia*, and one might nearly say only the *Oresteia*, presents the latter possibility. Here the heroic, active world of Orestes, Apollo, and Athena is successfully reconciled with the revenging, re-active world of the Furies. The world is made whole. This seems like an act of the strongest optimism, yet to describe it as such does it little justice. In the first place, it devalues the price paid in blood for the closing unanimity. The scream of Cassandra is not silenced by the final processional, nor does it seem unimportant by comparison, but rather that suffering, and the suffering of Agamemnon, Orestes, and Clytemnestra, keeps the conclusion from an *ex machina* facility. So too, tragedies with disastrous endings are just as optimistic as the *Oresteia*, and the *Oresteia* is equipped with just as complete a pessimism as theirs. Tragedy depends upon a balance between these poles. We might call this element "compensation," a phenomenon by which every misfortune has a positive by-product, and by which every triumph is paid for in full with suffering. A hero dies; but this means that a hero has lived. A contradiction is reconciled; and we count the dead.

Most tragedies, then, are dramas with unhappy endings. But to see this generalization as central or normative to the nature of the problem is self-destructive, particularly in the study of tragedy since 1800. The generic assertion is damaging since it disallows an empirical recognition of change, and the assertion about endings causes a distortion in critical emphasis. In fact, it is curiously true that almost any simple claim made for tragedy as a whole leads to similar misunderstandings and misplaced emphases. For every aspect of the problem that we expect to yield a norm, we find another paradox, until we begin to suspect that paradox itself is the only norm. What becomes important, then, is not the fact of paradox so much as the places in which it is found. To a great extent the definition of the tragic tradition depends upon this realization.

Consider, for example, the question of tragic language. We read Aristotle's discussion of the element of "thought" as if it were a unified proposition. But it is not so. Tragedy from its origins possesses a language divided against itself, a fusion of choric, collective utterance and the more uniform, individual meters of the epic tradition. The first actor, a development from choric verse said to have taken place in the sixth century in the plays of Thespis, apparently did not use the same language as did the chorus from which he arose. He spoke in iambic trimeter, or an ancestor thereof, while the chorus ordered its songs according to strophe, antistrophe, and epode rather than according to any metric line in particular. When we read of the physical change involved in the advent of this first actor, we are also considering an evolving dichotomy of speech. The character who individuates himself must function as a focal point, a narrator of a singular and unique series of events, distinguishing himself from the cyclic relationships of man to god and earth with which the chorus is concerned. By the time of the *Eumenides*, the dialectic of speech had flowered into contrasting modes of life and thought. They are related to the poles of Achilles' choice: Should one live briefly as a completely defined individual? Or should one only endure in the timeless anonymity in which life, love, and death are passed as burdens from generation to generation—but in which even such burdens are a cause for exhilaration?

The paradoxes of the tragic tradition always radiate in this way. The apparently ethical and social fusion that takes place at the end of the *Oresteia* is also a prophecy about language: that the diction of the stage shall be eternally wedded to the diction of the chorus, that dance and song will not exist in this tradition without rhetoric. Still, the fusion leaves a vast flexibility. Stage language may be as honest as Orestes, as just as Athena, as manipulative as Apollo. Choric language, without the burden of action upon it, need not be forever public as must the speech of a god who cannot escape the strong light that falls ceaselessly across his mask. It can collectivize private reaction, paradoxically, into a thing as public as mass song.

Certain of these paradoxes, of course, seem to have only a historical validity. Why, for example, did the chorus vanish from the stage? Perhaps, as man becomes more sophisticated, he demands increasingly indirect statements of truth. Although we may feel as vigorously involved in the world and its variety as we did in adolescence, we no longer read the authors who once spoke so well to early appetite. On the one hand, this is a sign of maturation in our tastes, but on the other hand it is a symptom of a jaded sensibility. The clarity and simplicity of construction in Greek theatre, with the chorus in the foreground and the actors rising singly above and behind them, may have come to express too much at once, too much religion, too much politics, ethics, aesthetics, linguistics, and emotion too directly. Like a metaphor heard too often, its justice may have waned into cliché. Without it, however, it is hard to see what continuity the Elizabethans could have seen between their serious drama and that of the Greeks. One can of course cite the study of Seneca in the schools, and the publication of university translations of Roman drama. But is there a deeper, more meaningful affinity?

For the Elizabethans, this is Achilles' choice:

Whether 'tis nobler in the mind to suffer
The slings and arrows of outrageous fortune,
Or to take arms against a sea of troubles,
And by opposing end them.

This is the premise in a number of Shakespeare's plays. Lear, seeking to retreat from the public light into the choric namelessness of his retainers; Hamlet, trapped between his songlike language and his sword; Macbeth, taunted by a witch-chorus into leaving a life of service for a dream of action, a hallucinated dagger. Now the choric impulse is released through other outlets: the comic scenes, with their anonymous, type-named characters, where the language of the masses is spoken, and where songs are sung. In the speech of the actors also, there are soliloquies which, as in classical choruses, stop the forward motion of events. Now it is the hero showing his reflective side; now it is no longer a structural metaphor of the theatre, but the brute fact of the disunity in every man. Where the Greeks' disjuncture could once, at least, be assembled into a processional of hope, now the contradiction is half joined, half sundered, like the co-existence of spirit and animal in the same form of man. Push and pull as they may, the two poles can never again be pure. For every assertion will come the inevitable and equal reaction of the other. The language of the streets meets the language of the courts on a single stage, and all strata of London society sit in hierarchical sections of the same house. Yet, this theatre fosters no Aeschylean feeling of national unity. It is a place more than slightly immoral to frequent, a place one forbids women to enter, a place that the church dream of spiritual sovereignty cannot endure.

"Drama flourishes best in the center of the life of its time," wrote Francis Fergusson, and this is hardly the simple statement it may seem at first glance. What be-

comes of the tragic tradition when it becomes the property of court society exclusively, even in a situation where
the court is the center of the life of its time? Characters
in Corneille and Racine describe their passions in mag-
nificent language. But that act itself, the enumeration
of feelings like the symptoms of a disease, belies the
veracity of their existence. If I am capable of analyzing
my overwhelming passion, then I am not truly over-
whelmed. For French Classical tragedy, reason is too
often the index of the irrational, emotion is seen as an
admirable but guilty departure from the norms of logical
behavior. Hence there is not only no chorus, there is
nothing that assumes its function. The interest in "higher"
mental operations is coincident with the limitation of
social interest to a tiny elite. From this follows a complete formalization into acts, until every plot is funda-
mentally the same. The definition of catastrophe is broad-
ened to include not only traditional forms of death and
blinding, but also in *Le Cid*, the act of entering a cloister.

The continuation of the tension between chorus and
stage depends upon universal accessibility to the work of
art. Only a potentially scoffing proletariat will prevent
the preening of the aristocracy and the abstract talk of
reason. Yet, say what we may, drama during the last
hundred and fifty years has moved even further from
"the center of the life of its time." Instead of forging a
new style, it has generally modelled itself on Athens,
London, or Paris of the great periods. This is certainly
true of Romantic drama, with Schiller interested mainly
in Shakespeare, Byron in Marlowe, and Shelley in Aeschylus. Now poetry and the novel are closer to the cen-

ter than drama, and all intent of performance disappears from works such as *Faust, Manfred*, and *Prometheus Unbound*. These works, remote descendants of *Samson Agonistes*, mark the end of the alliance between tragedy and the stage, and if tragedy has a theatre thereafter, it is often the theatre of a single mind confronting the work of art in privacy.

But this does not mean that the choric element disappears. Interestingly enough, there is always an equivalent tension of language in works that owe large debts to the tragic tradition. When Kleist, Melville, or Faulkner uses a strange syntax, it is sometimes an echo of something old and dark and oracular. As long as the work of art remains verbal, there can be a choric counterpart, a rebirth of the paradox. This affirms the importance of words to tragedy, and ought to be enough refutation for those who feel that tragedy has broken free of literature and now circulates freely as "the Tragic." For only words can give form to the choice of Achilles and all its emotional concomitants. Tragedy can take place only in literary worlds, since its language must be regarded as more than a tool for communication. There is, in brief, no tragedy without poetry of one kind or another. This is an example—and only one example—of a genuine tragic norm.

Criticism of tragedy needs to make a compromise between a purely historical and purely formalistic understanding of the tradition. One may interject at this point that Hegel has already accomplished this, or that Nietzsche's *Birth of Tragedy* has provided the necessary tools.

Yet it is curiously true that there exists an overriding dialectic between these two dialecticians. Hegel is ultimately rational, so that his analysis of tragedy is dependent largely on the action as it is played by stage-figures in classical drama. The famous critique of the *Antigone* is really a highly sophisticated examination of the relationship of named characters as abstract ethical absolutes, confronting each other on the surface of the action, the plot. Nietzsche, on the other hand, assigns the dialectical tension to the opposition of stage-figures and chorus, a contrast of larger modes which makes the antagonism of the characters seem superficial by comparison. Hegel's method depends on linear and temporal factors, like a syllogism; but Nietzsche's is atemporal since the relationship of chorus and characters is the same at any moment of the play, and is fixed that way by the very origins, by the birth of tragedy itself.

The most sensible attitude toward these two theorists is that they are both necessary, though neither is in himself sufficient, to a thorough understanding of tragedy. It may at first glance seem impossible to combine their insights fruitfully, since Hegel saw the irrational as simply unreal, while Nietzsche saw reason as having no place in tragedy—as, in fact, the external power that came in time to destroy it. What is at stake is more than a choice between historicism and formalism. In twentieth-century criticism the choice involves taking sides on the debate of origins, between the Nietzschean Cambridge Anthropological School on the one hand, and Pickard-Cambridge and Gerald Else on the other. It affects the critic's interpretation of the meaning of order and disorder, which is at the heart of the question, and it affects the method by which he decides which disputable works may be regarded as tragedies and which may not. For these reasons, it is probably worth while to go into the implications of the decision a little more deeply.

To understand what Hegel's theory of tragedy is lacking demands an understanding of the logical basis for his analysis. Tragedy results from the collision of two characters, each of whom becomes identical with some ethical concept. The confrontation of Creon and Antigone, then, is in fact the same as a jurisdictional dispute between the State and the Family, each of which is legitimate and possesses, in Hegelian terms, a portion of Absolute ethical substance. The problem then becomes similar to the question in physics of what takes place when an irresistible force meets an immovable object. Either both will be destroyed, or one of the two will compromise its absoluteness and cease to be either irresistible or immovable. The latter solution Hegel regards as somehow illegitimate, involving a compromise of the essence that gives tragedy its sense of cosmic importance. On these grounds he dismisses the *Oresteia* itself. In the *Antigone* he finds his ideal example of the uncompromising clash of absolutes, to the destruction of both.

Not only does this theory undermine the human quality of tragic art, making it instead a scientific or even pedantic war of abstractions; it also reduces the importance of all but one of the Aristotelian elements, until that one, action, becomes the all-in-all. But what sort of action is it? Not really a Homeric battle of heroes, but rather action in the manner of progress through a syllogism.

The Absolute exists.
The Absolute does not exist.

The Absolute is becoming.

In this form, Hegel tells us, all human knowledge comes into the world. The process is called *negation*, but paradoxically it is the most positive force in the cosmos. Across its abstract "time," the Absolute Spirit slowly comes to consciousness in the world. Therefore, everything that takes place in its progress is by definition good, so that at the end of a tragedy we are supposed to write off the losses to a generalized feeling of betterment and progress. It is indeed a "ghostly paradigm," which seems a million miles from the emotional intensity we associate with tragic art.

And yet the theory is vital in that it emphasizes the sort of balance that has to exist in a tragic action. The notion of equality of antagonists is the most important since it allows the distinction between tragedy and pathos, hence the difference between a tragic hero and a victim. For example, it has us understand that Antigone has a positive power all her own, that she is not a mere sacrifice to Creon's anger. Going beyond Hegel himself, we see that there are other reciprocities as well. With an almost medieval sense of justice, tragedy always balances loss with gain, gain with loss. He who is destroyed will always assert some positive attribute that will make him larger, more intense. He who appears victorious will always pay a bitter price for it. Thus, although Antigone dies she *does* carry with her a heightened sort of ethical purity, and Creon, although he is alive and ruling at the end of the play, has paid for survival with the destruction of his family.

Furthermore, Hegel helps us to clarify the idea of destiny in tragedy. He tells us that the characters are both individuals and delegates of some facet of the Absolute. Now this indicates that they are neither entirely free to act as they please, nor are they totally controlled by a superior force, for then they would be mere puppets. Hence we are able to discover the middle-ground between free will and necessity that is at the heart of Greek literature in general, the tenet that destiny is so closely linked with the self that simply by *living it out* the self will complete and fulfill it. Students of grammar are aware that in certain languages, among them Greek, there exists a verbal expression between the active and the passive voices which is known as the median or middle. At times this is a mere paradox of grammar, like the humorous quirks that occur in the assignment of nominal gender; at other times, it has a reflexive sense. But there is also a class of verbs in which a middle-ground exists. Consider *dunamai*, "to be able." What is ability? In one sense, it is something that is within us, that we hold passively. On the other hand, it is a type of potential energy, containing if not action at least the promise of action. It is within this unique middle-ground that we find tragic fate. The protagonist does what he does neither because he is forced to, nor because it is all his own idea. Vaster currents are moving. Conceivably he could avoid them. We can imagine—remotely—Achilles opting to return to his anonymous and lengthy life. *But then he would not be Achilles.* The decision that he makes becomes himself, becomes what he is. In this sense the elusive notion of fate is closer to the concept of character. It is reflected in the reciprocity between the tragic hero as individual and as leader of a nation or race. For although he may lean toward one pole or the other, there is never a completely defined dichotomy between the public and the private man. And this is what Hegel means by the world-historical individual.

The insufficiency of Hegel's theory stems from the fact that he is almost entirely concerned with the stage figures, to the exclusion of the chorus. There is no question that Nietzsche was overcompensating for this in *The Birth of Tragedy* by asserting the historical primacy of the chorus, and by calling the stage characters mere dreams that arise like ghosts from the choric energy. Just as clearly, he is reacting against the sort of plot analysis that Hegel's action-oriented thesis stimulates. The identification of the chorus with ancient and irrational Dionysian mysteries is certainly the most daring stroke of critical counterthrust in the nineteenth century. No amount of analysis ever explained the emotional power of tragedy so well. There is no more syllogism, and all action, being hallucinated, is compressed into the verticality of emotive time. The dialectic is not merely something acted out, but is essential to the very structure of the drama, even the structure of the stage on which it is performed.

At first glance it is tempting to see Nietzsche's dialectic as identical with the dialectic between *Odyssey* and *Iliad*, with the Apollonian as the heroes' mode of existence (*Iliad*), and the Dionysian as the centripetal mode of the chorus (*Odyssey*). Although there is a sort of subjective correctness to this alignment, when examined closely there is a divergence that will cause trouble unless

it is clarified at the outset. In Nietzsche the term Dionysian is associated with a primal, demonic power that is
celebrated in music and the dance. We see the image
of the patron god wreathed with ivy, unashamed of cor-
poreality and its potential violence. He is the Antichrist
toppling the pretense of ethical systems with a shot of
his eyes, collapsing the castle of Pentheus with a wave
of the hand. We recognize him as the wanderer, returning to Greece full of exoticism gathered from exile in the
East, recruiting followers into his illegal mysteries. Not
only Antichrist but Anarchist, he is a political threat to
the aristocrats and their Olympian gods, returning to a
clean theology the grotesque immediacy of revelation.

On the other hand, following Nietzsche we see the
other, Apollonian pole as purely dream, a sensual but
static manifestation of the individual as opposed to the
universality of the Dionysian. "Und so war, überall dort,
wo das Dionysische durchdrang, das Apollonische auf-
gehoben und vernichtet."[1] ("And so, wherever the Dionysian prevailed, the Apollonian was checked and destroyed.")[2] "Apollo aber tritt uns wiederum als die
Vergöttlichung des principii individuationis entgegen, in
dem allein das ewig erreichte Ziel des Ur-Einen, seine
Erlösung durch den Schein, sich vollzieht."[3] ("Apollo,
however, again appears to us as the apotheosis of the
principium individuationis, in which alone is consummated the perpetually attained goal of the primal unity,

---

[1] Friedrich Nietzsche, *Gesammelte Werke*, 3er band, München,
1920, p. 39.
[2] Friedrich Nietzsche, *The Birth of Tragedy and The Care of
Wagner*, trans. Walter Kaufmann, New York, 1967, p. 47.
[3] Nietzsche, *Gesammelte Werke*, 3er band, p. 37.

its redemption through mere appearance.")[4] We see the principle most vividly, according to Nietzsche, in Doric art, the sort for which people employ the adjective "serene." Here all is formal, fixed like hallucination, hence dreamlike and without energy. This hardly corresponds to the types of heroism we see in tragedy. Between these and the Apollonian figures on the Parthenon stretches an abyss as wide as that between the orgiastic Dionysos and the stern, moralistic Furies of the *Oresteia*.

Does it make sense, then, to use the Nietzschean terms at all, or should we be content with a dialectic between *Iliad* and *Odyssey*, the choice that Achilles made and the one he did not? It might be objected that the foregoing view of Nietzsche so inverts his terminology that it is confusing to maintain it. There are several justifications, however. First of all, these concepts in their original form have had widespread currency among literary practitioners, writers as important as Gide, Mann, and Faulkner. Of course, as original artists these men too made significant modifications of the terms. For all that, however, they have contributed to the nearly popular status that Apollo and Dionysos enjoy at the present time. Since our grounds for realignment are empirical, it will be necessary to make local changes in the words whenever we use them. The same would have to be true of any terms we might substitute.

Second, there is a historical context in which the evolution of the terms may be placed. By the time of Peisistratos and the construction of the city Dionysia, the Dionysian religion was organized into a real political

[4] Nietzsche, *The Birth of Tragedy and The Case of Wagner*, p. 45.

force, one that the first great tyrant needed to harness and co-opt in order to gain and hold power. It is impossible to envision his *coup d'état* as a revolution of wreathed, half-naked revelers. Rather, the god whom Jane Harrison called the *eniautos daimon*, or seasonal god, became associated with the passing of the year not only for ritualistic purposes but also in relation to the practical knowledge of the earth and climate that a farmer needed to survive. Dionysos became emblematic of all the economic and political demands made by this farming class on the city of Athens proper. By the time of the *Oresteia*, we see the Furies not as amoral, but as alternatively moral, as strict and unyielding proponents of a direct and violent justice. Like radicals of any era, they find in the court of Athena an establishmentarian institution being used to treat insurgency according to the establishment's own forms. Like that of the Puritan rebels of the English seventeenth century, their anger has an ascetic righteousness. Punishing violence with violence, they still see restoration of order as an aim, they are still creatures of the earth and the fertile soil. They move in a chorus like the ancient revelers of their ancestry, they stand for the same notions of collectivity as opposed to individuation, yet now their old relish of disorder has as its end the order of the hearth, the seasons of planting and harvest. Nietzsche sees them as the disorderly source of all life and energy, but he fails to recognize that when absorbed by masses of people this energy takes form and generates an order of its own, so that when we see the Dionysian as irrational in modern tragedy, this does not mean that it is formless. In post-classical times, Dionysian characters are not revelers, but are still

choric in the sense that they represent a larger communality of experience, the anonymous labor, reflection and
reaction that characterize the sensitive unheroic men with
whom the world is most generally populated. Thus we
have a Horatio, an Ishmael, a Quentin Compson, not creatures of license and disorder, but delegates of the order
of compassion, reflection, survival, and affirmation—and
suffering. In modern tragedy, this is what we mean by
Dionysian.

So too with the Apollonian. Their illusory nature and
dreamlike lack of energy do not stand up under investi-
gation. Rather, we find in the ranks of Apollonians those
who have brought individual heroism to its utmost.
Against the lonely but passionate comfort of the Dionysian as we have reinterpreted it, they lift their visionary—
but not illusory—orders. While the choric voices call at
them constantly, offering decent and honorable lives of
obscurity, their energy surges ahead. They have about
them an uncompromising power, a revolutionary idea
of another world which they intrude violently into the
standing order. In short, modern tragedy brings a certain reversal of the roles. The Dionysian is no longer the
source of energy. It does not act to bring forth the spec-
ters of individuality, but rather *re*acts to them when they
come. It is no longer the rebellious and disorderly power,
but rather—one is tempted to say since the incorporation
of the Eumenides into the mainstream of city life—it is
the standing order toward which the Apollonians are
revolutionary. Tragedy still depends, as Nietzsche said
it did, on their common presence and opposition, but it
no longer occurs as he said it did. From ancient revelers
modern Dionysians gain their compassion and integrity,

their commitment to the life of the heart rather than of the mind. So too from mythic heroes modern Apollonians acquire an atmosphere of the large and unending, even as their piteously certain mortality is enacted before us over and over again. The categories are still helpful, if we see that they have evolved from the primitive forms to which Nietzsche gives so much—indeed too much— consideration. They are still useful as a kind of short-hand, then, to suggest the broader cultural dialectic of which tragedy is only the most brilliant and complete manifestation. We need Hegel to understand the heroic half, and Nietzsche to understand the rest. Through these two philosophers, the dialectic of Greece was brought vividly into our century. Inexorably, we can understand Greece in no other way. However we alter and revise, we owe the philosophers some of the immediacy of Aeschylus.

Neither Hegel nor Nietzsche wrote tragedy; they only wrote about it. This is because each is interested exclusively in one pole of the dualism. The men who write tragedy are distinguished by an almost involuntary com-prehension of the alternatives in their full range. Hence Aeschylus was drawn to Pythagoras, who spoke of *krasis*, or the mixing of opposites into the *harmonia* of the uni-verse. He must have relished Pythagoras' use of reason to achieve mystical insight, the balance he spoke of as necessary to a good life, his harnessing of Dionysian elements under the patronage of Apollo. The *Oresteia* can be seen as a dramatization of the agonizing attain-ment of this *harmonia* in society as a whole. In Shake-speare it takes the form of an opposition between the rising commercial and legal ethics of the day and the vestiges of Medieval Christianity. And in the tragedy of modern times a whole selection of orders is pitted against a plethora of anti-establishmentarian doctrines. In part, this is a healthy multiplicity resulting from the rise of individualism, in part it is an uncertainty that has brought about periods of brief and intense cataclysm separated by uneasy peacetimes. But it has become more and more difficult to differentiate personal and cultural contradictions. To be dislodged from order no longer requires a relish for Dionysian emotion. It may result entirely from the affirmative claims of rival orders. People bemoan the lack of heroes when in fact the problem is that there are too many different kinds. They say that the world lacks tragic possibilities when in fact there are so many that they have become pitfalls. In order to find modern tragedy, we must discard the notion that there is one central kind. We do not have a Dionysia or a Globe Theatre. We must settle for local dialectics with universal vibrations. This is nothing more than a response to the decentralization of ideology.

2 *A Case of Migration through Genres*

///

Ihr last gewiss ein griechisch Trauerspiel?
In dieser Kunst möcht ich was profitieren,
Denn heutzutage wirkt das viel.

(Faust, Part I, 523-525)

The relationship of *Faust* to the tragic tradition is engaging for two reasons. First, it is a consideration on the highest level of the question of redemptive tragedy; second, it addresses itself to the problem of tragedy and genre in a very explicit way. The fact that, in spite of its subtitle, it may not itself be a tragedy is of tertiary concern here. The initial impressiveness of the work stems from its attempt to hold the same position in nineteenth-century tragedy that the *Oresteia* held in Athens—as a statement of both unification and universality that would function as both a fountainhead and a culmination of the literature of its time.

If epic poems characteristically begin *in medias res*, tragedies begin *in extremis*. When we want to investigate a work's place in the tradition, the opening often provides an important first clue. We discover, for example, that the *Prometheus* opens in Scythia, at the farthest boundary of the known world; that the *Oresteia* starts at the extreme end of the war; that *Oedipus Coloneus* begins at the uttermost point of the old man's wanderings;

that Euripides' *Electra* commences in the outlands of the kingdom, at the nadir of the heroine's humiliation. These external aspects are really only symptoms, however, of a deeper extremity, the feeling that an order of the world is at an end, or that the last mitigations of a confrontation between two orders are being removed. It is like the crisis of a disease. Either death or recovery—but no further suspension of a state between the two—will be indicated very soon.

This extreme condition is usually reflected in the situation which provides the starting point for the action, and I will return to this point often in the subsequent chapters. *Faust*, however, opens with another sort of extreme conflict. An elitist poet is confronted with the demands of a popularizing stage manager. The result is a dialectic of genres that announces the curious middle ground in which the work is to operate. Although Goethe respects the "pure" poet as the source of the work, the apparent victor in the dispute is the stage manager along with his ally the jester. Goethe, of course, worked for twenty-six years as a director, at the same time writing lyric poetry, so that the first prologue is something of a personal declaration. Yet in spite of the stage manager's victory, *Faust* is not a performable drama.

It must be noted that this paradox of form is not new with Goethe. Contemplation of it leads to several profound questions about the true function of poetry in the world. One entails meditation on the prehistoric oral origins of poetry, and the changes wrought by its transformation into a written medium. Another and related one is the question of the chorus, its religious origins and its various modern incarnations, which I shall try to deal with in a later chapter. But even the purely generic problem of an unperformable drama precedes *Faust*. The example that comes most readily to mind is *Samson Agonistes*, where Milton, in his effort to write in English an example of each of the classical modes, comes to tragedy as if it were as consummately literary as the pastoral. Milton counted on the sheer resonance of his verse to force a transition from the visual to the aural, but his total remove from dramaturgy necessitates the degree of abstraction from immediate theatre which his detractors have termed academic. Milton's work, however, has never become the specimen in a bottle that one might have expected. Its influence is clearly felt in other generic hybrids of the Romantic period, in England particularly *Manfred*, *Prometheus Unbound*, and, later, Beddoes' *Death's Jest-Book*. These pieces form a collection of transitional moments, mid-points in evolution that foreshadow more elaborate changes.

The main release afforded a writer of non-dramatic plays is that he is excused from theatrical *timing*. There is more room to expound on the historical, philosophical or political implications of the conflict of orders. No one can be blind to the relationship between, for example, *Samson* and the Puritan rebellion. The problem with such pieces, especially the Romantic ones, is that they do not develop an alternative timing scheme. In brief, they ramble, since they are excused from the demand for condensation that produces a Shakespearean soliloquy. Action can be de-emphasized as the primary unifying force of the work. Instead, as in *Faust*, they are permitted to begin on an extreme of literary ideology.

Unperformable drama is too unstable a compound ever

to evolve its own behavioral or formal laws. Since tragedy is primarily a pattern of literary action, it seems, in retrospect, inevitable that tragedy would migrate to another genre whose tradition contained well-established exigencies of timing and action. Clearly, the novel—or else the shorter forms of prose fiction—comes to mind immediately. Certainly Byron was aware of this transition in *Manfred*. But no one was quite so conscious of it as was Goethe, who, like Milton, operated in so many genres and understood them all. The episodic nature of the plot of *Faust* can only recall *Don Quixote* and other picaresque tales. The hero and his ever-present companion also seem to owe something to Cervantes. Similarly, the Gothic elements, the open form, and, above all, the humor are much more closely related to contemporary fiction than to contemporary drama. In these respects, a comparison with Schiller would be revealing. Schiller's firm adherence to the norms of tragedy is exemplary. He presents a conflict brought to extremes from the start; employs measures to assure that the two poles of the conflict are equally asserted (though his own favoritism in *Maria Stuart*, for one, is evident); employs the critical moment of tragic choice, and the classical development of heroism to the border of madness. Where Schiller, however, did not call *Maria Stuart* a tragedy, perhaps because of his favoritism, he did call it a play. Goethe, on the other hand, called *Faust* a tragedy but not a drama, and this is an important moment in the history of our tradition.

Goethe once remarked that there was something in him that was antithetical to the truly tragic. This means, on one level, that there was a part of his nature that had

confidence in the ultimate negotiability of human conflict. Thus we see early in *Faust* that the devil and the
Lord are not on particularly bad terms. Each seems willing to accept the other for what he is. In the apparently
dualistic universe in which the action takes place, there
is a kind of rivalry of light and dark powers, but no out-
right clashes. There is a distinct similarity between the
spirits of the Classical Walpurgis Night and the spirits
that figure in the redemptive display at the end of Part II.
There is symmetry, rather than negation, between the
divine and the diabolic. They are comparable, not com-
petitive.

For all that, however, there *is* a genuine dialectic to be
found in *Faust*, a conflict that resembles the tragic just
enough to align the work with the tradition. This is the
tension between Faust's humanity and his desire for absolute knowledge. This self-division turns up again and
again in modern tragedy. Into a human world—and, as it
turns out, a superhuman world—condemned to the finite,
comes a man who has a vision of an order infinite and
absolute. His mind surges ahead of time, and can never
be content with stasis. So given to this order is Faust,
and so confident of its ultimate triumph, that he is willing
to wager his soul on it. The pact with the devil, for all
its humor, is the moment of choice.

It is not a particularly affecting instance of tragic
choice, though, since it happens early in the work and
thus resembles a premise more than a leap of commitment. The hesitation of Orestes is not present, nor even
that of Maria Stuart. Either we see Faust as inhumanly
obsessed, and lose touch with his progress toward that
obsession, or else we feel that we are not supposed to

take the whole thing quite seriously. The latter suspicion is reinforced as the action progresses. For no matter how extreme Faust becomes in his personal order, there is no pattern of events that draws him inevitably closer to a confrontation between that order and any other order. And therefore the play does not begin *in extremis*. It begins as if it had plenty of time. And of course, it does.

It would be a distortion, I think, to argue that *Faust* is *primarily* a disquisition on tragedy. Yet such a disquisition is one of its major elements, to the point where it is possible to find oneself thinking of it as a theoretical rather than practical work. The scene called "Trüber Tag" and the two following scenes employ the Mannerist timing of *Macbeth* in an exemplary fashion. So too, we find Shakespearean soliloquies and low comic interludes. On the other hand, there are scenes which might well be translated from some lost Greek manuscript, like the third act of Part II. The traditional Greek rhythm of speeches, choruses, and *stichomythia* passages is remarkably well captured. Yet the very unperformability of the piece makes these elements seem like examples, like deliberate virtuosities. Similar questions come to mind concerning the ending. There is a sense in which it is a statement against tragedy and in favor of synthesis from above. In this context it becomes a credo for a humanistic age. Here the resemblance to the *Oresteia* is obvious, yet the difference is notable as well.

The main defense of the *Oresteia* as tragedy hinges on the compensatory suffering which has occurred throughout the earlier portions of the trilogy. The resolution constitutes a re-ordering of the universe, a sort of fresh start. It does not have a *post facto* side. It does not try to assuage the spirits of the dead by forgetting them. The integrity of the Eumenides forbids that, so that even the resolution is harrowing. In *Faust*, however, the administration of a drug to induce amnesia at the start of the second part seems antithetical to a tragic pattern of action. Even the apparition of Gretchen among the hosts welcoming Faust to heaven seems to be under the spell of forgetfulness, unlike Virgil's meeting of Dido and Aeneas in the underworld. Faust's end might be likened more closely to the apotheosis of Oedipus in the *Coloneus*, and indeed the sense of forgiveness is common to them. But then the problem becomes largely stylistic. When Oedipus disappears from the earth, there is something terrible in this act of absolution from beyond, but in Goethe it has a musical-comedy atmosphere that in effect calls off any continuation of human suffering.

Faust is one of those works of literature that attempt to summarize and thus end the tradition to which they belong. *Don Juan* attempts to do much the same thing for epic heroism, and, much later of course, Nietzsche will try to do away with philosophy, Joyce with the novel, and Beckett with drama. Although none of these attempts has entirely succeeded, they have served to stun successors into silence for a while. Perhaps *Faust* has something to do with the remainder of the century and its failure to produce dramatic tragedy. In any event, whether through negative or positive example, *Faust* is important for the migration of genres that tragedy is to undergo, for, as a celebration of order in the cosmos, it drives tragedy, which is a celebration of paradox, into precincts less strongly governed by its influence—into, for example, the traditional German species called the *Novelle*.

Michael Kohlhaas, like other *Novellen* of the period, possesses a curious fusion of the moral and supernatural. Kleist's most immediate ancestor in the form is, not surprisingly, Goethe, whose examples in that genre, according to E. K. Bennett, emphasize "a moralizing element which is alien to the Novelle in its original form. . . . This moralizing element . . . is developed by Goethe to the furthest extent which is compatible with the form of the Novelle as a genre, and with him this particular type of Novelle comes to an end." Yet, Bennett goes on, Kleist used the term "moralische Erzählungen" to refer to his productions in the form, "not that they convey a moral as Goethe's Novellen do—but in this sense that they propound moral problems with which not only the principal but sometimes the subsidiary characters have to deal. Generally, the problems are insoluble."[1] Again, Goethe is inescapable, yet here his hold is less rigid. Kleist designed his challenge to Goethe with two tactics: first, by a return to interest in the ordinary; second, almost paradoxically, by a return to interest in the historical.

But an even more important arena for Kleist is simply that of language. He shares with Aeschylus a language tortured into difficulty by the stress of contradiction in the action. With fragmentation, ellipsis, oversized vocabulary, and neologism, Aeschylus weighs every syllable with a burden of significance. Kleist's long, spun sentences, his archaism and legalism, achieve the effect of diffusion of meaning across longer periods of time. In the condensed language of Aeschylus, time is foreshortened, and the past which the archaisms suggest comes

[1] Bennett, E. K., *A History of the German Novelle*, Cambridge, 1961, pp. 36-37.

into the present as a living force. In Kleist, where action seems almost to take place in spite of the language, the past becomes a gloom through which we strain to see small figures moving. In any event, it is a reaction against the balanced language of moralizing in Goethe, and it is a tribute to the vitality of the younger man that the older one never had anything kind to say about his work.

The contradiction is almost as hopeless as it is simple. Kohlhaas is one of the most upright (*rechtschaffensten*) men of his time, and is also one of the most abominable (*entsetzlichsten*). Here, without the Faustian insistence upon the cosmic, Kleist reaches after the absolute. Kohlhaas is identified with absoluteness of the individual, the Elector with the absoluteness of the state. Like Maria Stuart and her cousin Elisabeth, they are somehow dependent upon each other. The Elector controls Kohlhaas' relationship to the government; the horse dealer, by virtue of the capsule that he wears around his neck, controls the Elector's identity as an individual. The two orders come to their inexorable collision, and both are destroyed. Kohlhaas, the initiator, injures innocent people in the name of a cause with which they are barely familiar. He plunges the countryside into civil war on the basis of a personal complaint. And yet, within the order he brings with him, he is rational, compassionate, and even sympathetic. He gives his opponents every chance to surrender before he comes to violence.

At the start, Kohlhaas is a bourgeois tradesman, the prosperous father of an exemplary family. He is part of the prevalent order of the world. When he first sees the Junker's tollgate, it is something that "er sonst auf diesem

Wege nicht gefunden hatte" (p. 9),[2] ("he never before had found on that road"). The world is somehow changing, but has the order diverged from Kohlhaas, or Kohlhaas from the order? Suddenly, in a moment that must have influenced Kafka, the horse dealer is asked to produce a pass which is now required of tradesmen crossing the border. He says, in good Kafkaesque language, "dass er, soviel er wisse, keinen habe" (p. 10), ("that he had none, so far as he knew"). In Dresden, where he goes to obtain the pass, he discovers that there is no such thing, that he has been a victim of a ruse to take some of his horses. The castellan, upon Kohlhaas' return, reports to the Junker that "dieser Rosskamm, weil seine Rappen ein wenig gebraucht worden wären, für eine Rebellion verführe" (p. 15), ("that this horse dealer, because his black horses had been used a little, was causing an uproar"). Even at this early date, before any thought of military uprising, Kohlhaas is already almost called a rebel.

Even as he is excluded from one order, he gains understanding of his own. His sense of Justice, likened to a gold scale, wavers as he makes careful inquiries before coming to total commitment. Almost from the start, this sense of justice is considered more than an individual mania.

Wenn der ganze Vorfall, wie es allen Anschein habe, bloss abgekartet sein sollte, er mit seinen Kräften der Welt in der Pflicht verfallen sei, sich Genugtuung für zukünftige seinen Mitbürgern zu vershaffen (p. 16).

[2] Von Kleist, Heinrich, *Sämtliche Werke und Briefe*, 2er band, München, 1961. All page references to this edition.

(If the whole incident, as seemed probable, should have been premeditated, he with all his power must get satisfaction for himself for the offense done him, and protect his fellow-citizens against future ones.)

At this very early point in the *Novelle*, the grievance already has an expanded significance. Later it will add to this social meaning a religious and political dimension.

The force of his resolution, after his legal rejection from Dresden, is expressed in this startling passage:

Und mitten durch den Schmerz, die Welt in einer so ungeheuren Unordnung zu erblicken, zuckte die innerliche Zufriedenheit empor, seine eigne Brust nunmehr in Ordnung zu sehen (p. 24).

(And through the pain of seeing the world in such vast disorder flashed an inner contentment at seeing his own heart now in order.)

Now Kohlhaas will proceed to sell his house and lands. The two conflicting orders are now fully defined, and fully irreconcilable. With the necessary exclusiveness, each sees the other as disorderly, evil. Correspondingly, the horse dealer's aims grow more universal as he becomes more absolute. He is prepared to throw over the notions of home and family so sacred to his class.

Kohlhaasenbrück sei ja nicht die Welt; es könne Zwecke geben, in Vergleich mit welchen, seinem Hauswesen, als ein ordentlicher Vater, vorzustehen, untergeordnet und nichtswürdig sei; und kurz, seine Seele, müsse er ihm sagen, sei auf grosse Dinge gestellt . . . (p. 25).

(Kohlhaasenbrück was certainly not the world; there could be aims in comparison with which to manage his household as an orderly father would be subsidiary and unworthy; in short, his soul, he must tell him that his soul was fixed upon great things. . . .)

Words like "ordentlicher" and "untergeordnet" are not used accidentally, for here Kohlhaas is defining the priorities of the new order he has come to embody. In terms of the legal bourgeois order, nothing is more sacred than house and kin, and indeed it is the very inviolability of family estates that allows the Junker to set up his toll-gate in the first place. It is the Junker's family connection with the court that keeps the law from passing any real judgment against him. The state, as Kleist sees it, is nothing but a collectivization of these landholders. Kohlhaas gladly belonged to this order at the start of the book —the town he lives in is named after his family, after all —but when his new order comes to realization the first thing he discards is domestic life. The death of Lisbeth gives this step an irreversibility. He will not see his children again until, under house arrest, he finds himself trying once again to operate within the established order of the state.

Lisbeth has died as the result of a blow from the butt of a lance dealt by a bodyguard of the Elector as she tried to present a petition from her husband. It is the first act of violence between the two orders, and it destroys the only character who could have played an intermediary role. She dies with her finger pointing to a verse from the Bible: "Vergib deinen Feinden; tue wohl auch denen, die dich hassen" (p. 30). ("Forgive your enemies; do good to those who hate you.") Kohlhaas gives her a funeral very different from that of an ordinary *bourgeoise*. "(Er) bestellte ein Leichenbegängnis, das weniger für sie, als für eine Fürstin, angeordnet schien" (p. 30). ("[He] ordered a funeral that was appropriate less for her than for a princess.") He is trying to make his alternative order equivalent to the state in some way, hence he gives her a kind of state funeral, as if he were actually sovereign of another kingdom. In perfectly logical continuation of this behavior, he issues his first manifesto on the day of the burial. This "Rechtsschluss" demands that the Junker return the horses and fatten them himself in Kohlhaas' stables. It is issued "kraft der ihm angeborenen Macht" (p. 31). ("By virtue of the power inborn in him.")

"Der Engel des Gerichts fährt also vom Himmel herab . . ." (p. 32). ("Thus the angel of judgment comes down from heaven.") This is how Kleist describes Kohlhaas' first attack on Castle Tronka. In a later manifesto, the horse dealer calls himself:

> einen Statthalter Michaels, des Erzengels, der gekommen sei, an allen, die in dieser Streitsache des Junkers Partei ergreifen würden, mit Feuer und Schwert, die Arglist, in welcher die ganze Welt versunken sei, zu bestrafen (p. 44).

> (a viceroy of the Archangel Michael who has come to punish all those who take the part of the Junker in this dispute with fire and sword, for the wickedness into which the whole world has sunk.)

He calls on the people to join him, to help him build "einer besseren Ordnung der Dinge" (p. 44), ("a better order of things"), and signs his mandates with the seal of the Provisionary World Government. Kohlhaas threatens the country with civil war.

Martin Luther is clearly doomed as an intermediary, since in a counter-manifesto he calls Kohlhaas' activities a "Selbstrache" or "personal revenge." The tone of the notice indicates that he is conscious of Kohlhaas only in an external way. The kernel of the interview between the theologian and the outlaw is contained in the following pronouncement of Kohlhaas:

> Der Krieg, den ich mit der Gemeinheit der Menschen führe, ist eine Missetat, sobald ich aus ihr nicht, wie Ihr mit die Versicherung gegeben habt, verstossen war (p. 45).

> (The war that I am waging against the society of men is a misdeed only so long as I have not been expelled from it, as you give me assurance I have not.)

The implication is that the horse dealer's actions are criminal only according to the rules of the standing order. Luther calls him "rasender, unbegreiflicher und entsetzlicher Mensch" (p. 46), ("mad, incomprehensible, and horrible man"). Yet Luther, although he does not understand Kohlhaas' world, does recognize its exclusivity:

> Kurz, dass man ihn, um aus dem Handel zu kommen, mehr als eine fremde, in das Land gefallene Macht, wozu er sich auch, da er ein Ausländer sei, gewissermassen qualifiziere, als einen Rebellen, der sich gegen den Thron auflehne, betrachten müsse (p. 49).

> (In brief, so as to settle the question, one should regard him more as a foreign power fallen upon the land

—he really might be so regarded, since he is a foreigner—rather than as a rebel against the throne.)

When Kohlhaas accepts the amnesty that Luther procures from the Elector, he gives up his claim to alternative statehood, but not his demands or his commitment to absolute justice. What disturbs him most, as the legalistic nets of the empire strangle him, is the show of justice they put on at the same time that they disregard the amnesty. In tragedy there must always be compensation. If Oedipus loses his kingdom and his sight, even as we are moved by the horror and the loss we are awed by the knowledge and vision he acquires in return. If Macbeth dies without a single objectively redeeming feature, still we do not feel mere relief at his destruction, but are impressed by his terrible vitality, and the forged agony of his language. Kleist gives Kohlhaas a very emblematic form of compensation, the capsule given him by a hag who turns out to be a reincarnation of his dead wife. This capsule contains a prophecy of the Elector's future, and gives him back an absoluteness powerful enough to compete with that of the state. State power imprisons the horse dealer, and the horse dealer imprisons the premier of the state. No amount of negotiation can reconcile the two. A promise of life and liberty, even granting the original demands, is not enough. The plea for his children sways him least of all.

What does the capsule signify? In part it is absolute justice, in part absolute individualism. But it must also be more than that, since it has the power to procure justice, and individual freedom, but Kohlhaas does not use it for either. One can only conclude that, having had a period of absolute commitment, Kohlhaas cannot part with absolutism itself. Having once set up a Provisional World Government, how is he to return to Kohlhaasenbrück and the life of a bourgeois tradesman? Kleist's tale is the tragedy of a man who, having known the absolutism of tragic heroism, is rendered unfit to go on living in the world.

3 *Tragedy in Prose Fiction:*
Moby-Dick

I have tried to show how the choice of Achilles came to be confronted by Michael Kohlhaas, a figure separated from the hero of the *Iliad* not only by time and space, but by genre as well. Kohlhaas, like Achilles, may leave his striving to return to his homeland, there to live long and prosperously. Remaining, each of the heroes surrenders longevity for the sake of intensity, giving his life form, individuality and uncompromised essence rather than anonymous survival among the mass of mankind.

What makes *Kohlhaas* peculiarly a work of the nineteenth century is its degree of abstraction. We can easily understand what glory awaits Achilles; it is the ancient distinction of prowess in battle, of making oneself physically and strategically superior to all others in the service of the *patria*. It carries with it an assurance of immortal fame, an eternal life rising from the strings and lips of bards. What compensation does Kohlhaas have to console him? At the end of the tale we are told that some descendants of the hero were still alive in Mecklenburg in the eighteenth century, but it says no more about them, nor does it indicate in any way that they were aware of their forefather. Eternal fame is not the motive, surely, nor is a desire to bestow fame on future generations, for the bestowal of infamy would be more likely. Surely the motive is partly a desire for revenge on the

Elector, but it is also more than that. Just as Achilles chooses to become the absolute hero, so Kohlhaas opts for absolute knowledge, made to seem more nearly absolute because of its abstraction and privacy even from the reader.

Kleist's prose tragedy is a "pure" example of the migration of genres, that is, the text itself makes no reference to dramatic form or to works of prior tragedians. All of its weaponry belongs to the arsenal of the *Novelle*. Yet the absolute nature of the hero's vision and self-vision, and the disorder that issues into the world as a result of it, are the very stuff from which tragedies are made. Either the hero must perish, or else the world would have to be fully reordered.

In *Moby-Dick* we are contending with a different sort of book. We now recognize it as an example of the American emblematic romance, perhaps its highest pinnacle. Yet at the time the book was written, the tradition that bore down upon the author was not so clearly defined as was the tradition of the *Novelle* out of which Kleist wrote. The tradition of nineteenth-century American fiction is our tradition, not Melville's. The author of *Moby-Dick* saw only Cooper as a literary ancestor, and hence felt quite free to employ any and all cultural sources he might encounter, from "Eschylus" (as he spelled it) through Bayle's dictionary to Emerson. Therefore, it is not surprising that he and his contemporaries lacked a novelistic conception of fiction. Without Richardson and Fielding as formal models, Melville was open to extra-novelistic interpolations in his works. Among these were dramatic scenes, such as the ones scattered throughout *Moby-Dick*. In order to understand in what more profound respects the novel belongs to the tragic legacy, it is first important to take account of these superficial affinities with drama.

The primary borrowing is from Shakespeare, whom Melville read assiduously just prior to the composition of *Moby-Dick*. There are several dramatically constructed scenes in the book, complete with stage directions, asides, and speaker headings. There are some twenty-odd soliloquies in which the debt to Shakespeare is particularly apparent. In one of these, we see Ahab raving at the lightning like Lear:

> I own thy speechless, placeless power; said I not so? Nor was it wrung from me; nor do I now drop these links. Thou canst blind; but I can then grope. Thou canst consume; but then I can be ashes. Take the homage of these poor eyes, and shutter-hands. I would not take it. The lightning flashes through my skull; mine eye-balls ache and ache; my whole beaten brain seems as beheaded, and rolling on some stunning ground. Oh, oh! Yet blindfold, yet will I talk to thee. Light though thou be, thou leapest out of the darkness; but I am darkness leaping out of light, leaping out of thee! The javelins cease; open eyes; see, or not? There burn the flames! Oh! thou magnanimous! now do I glory in my genealogy. But thou art but my fiery father; my sweet mother, I know not. Oh, cruel! what hast thou done with her? There lies my puzzle; but thine is greater, Thou knowest not how came ye, hence callest thyself unbegotten; certainly knowest not thy beginning, hence callest thyself unbegun. I know that

of me, which thou knowest not of thyself, oh, thou
omnipotent. There is some unsuffusing thing beyond
thee, thou clear spirit, to whom all thy eternity is but
time, all thy creativeness mechanical. Through thee,
thy flaming self, my scorched eyes do dimly see it.
Oh, thou foundling fire, thou hermit immemorial, thou
too hast thy incommunicable riddle, thy unparticipated
grief. Here again with haughty agony, I read my sire.
Leap! leap up, and lick the sky! I leap with thee; I
burn with thee; would fain be welded with thee; de-
fyingly I worship thee! (p. 417)[1]

Clearly, the language and syntax of this passage are
Shakespearean. The rhetorical questioning, the ungainly
metaphors ("my whole beaten brain seems as beheaded"), the word-play growing out of a basic dichotomy
like light and darkness, the placing of adjectives at times
after the nouns to which they refer, the use of unconven-
tional compound words such as "unsuffusing," and so
on. But more than just language allies the speech with
that of Lear on the moor in act 3, scene ii of that play.

> *Lear*: Blow, winds, and crack your cheeks! rage!
> blow!
> You cataracts and hurricanoes, spout
> Till you have drench'd our steeples, drown'd the
> cocks!
> You sulphurous and thought-executing fires,
> Vaunt-couriers to oak-cleaving thunderbolts,

---

[1] Herman Melville, *Moby-Dick*, ed. Harrison Hayford and
Hershel Parker, New York, 1967. All page references to this edition.

Singe my white head! And thou, all-shaking thunder,
Strike flat the thick rotundity o' the world!
Crack nature's moulds, all germens spill at once
That make ingrateful man!

· · · · · · · · · · · · · · · · · · · ·

   Rumble thy bellyful! Spit, fire! Spout, rain!
Nor rain, wind, thunder, fire, are my daughters:
I tax you not, you elements, with unkindness;
I never gave you kingdom, call'd you children,
You owe me no subscription: then, let fall
Your horrible pleasure; here I stand, your slave,
A poor, infirm, weak, and despis'd old man.
But yet I call you servile ministers,
That have with two pernicious daughters join'd
Your high-engender'd battles 'gainst a head
So white and old as this. O! O! 'tis foul.

The storm arouses in each of the protagonists not only
awe at the brilliance of the phenomenon but also thoughts
of paternity. Lear first relishes the brutal impartiality of
the elements, directed not just against him but against
the entire world. In this the storm differs from his daughters. Then, as the speech progresses, he comes to see the
lightning and thunder as mere agency, a power controlled
by his daughters to humiliate and torment him further.
In a similar way Ahab sees the storm not as the terror he
has begotten, but as the terror that has begotten him. He
sees it as an agency just as Lear does, but not an agency
of anything human; rather, it becomes the appearance of
a diabolical sort of absolute "to whom all thy eternity is
but time." The passages share a rhetorical elementality
appropriate to the natural violence. The great difference

between them—which is the difference of their times—
is that Lear sees the potential of the storm directed against
actual things—steeples, weathercocks, and, more cosmi-
cally, the shape of the world itself—but Ahab sees all its
violence as internal, speaks of the pain *within* his head,
says that his "brain seems as beheaded."

Without specific analogy to any one Shakespearean
hero, Ahab shares qualities of many of them. If he stands
in relation to the elements as Lear does, he stands in the
place of Macbeth in relation to the hierarchy of his ship.
Like Othello, he owes his high social place to ability
rather than heredity, and he has his Iago in the Parsee. It
is important, however, to notice that any of these resem-
blances would seem forced and arbitrary were it not for
the tone of the language. We will return to this point
later in greater detail. It is worth noting now, however,
that the relationship between a modern writer in English
and Shakespeare is in general more natural than an alliance between a modern and an ancient Greek. We use
many of the same words as the Elizabethans, though
meaning and orthography are certainly different. As we
look for things Greek in modern tragedy we hope to discover matters more subtle, more profound, and hopefully
more surprising. Charles Olson notes that " in the same
place where the notes for *Moby-Dick* are written in
his Shakespeare, Melville jots down: 'Eschylus Tragedies.' "[2]

Here the antecedent is less obvious, for it is not clear
to which tragedies of Aeschylus he might be referring.
Neither is it clear what translation of the texts Melville

[2] Charles Olson, *Call Me Ishmael*, New York, 1947, p. 58.

might have used, and these lacunae in our knowledge should not be taken lightly, since they render any correlation highly speculative. There is, however, a near-soliloquy, near-chorus in which Ishmael says, "God help thee, old man, thy thoughts have created a creature in thee; and he whose intense thinking thus makes him a Prometheus; a vulture feeds upon that heart for ever; that vulture is the very creature he creates" (p. 175). Indeed, *Moby-Dick* and the *Prometheus* are similarly elemental. The Titan, chained to rock (earth) high in the air, is famous as the giver of fire. To complete the traditional four elements, there is the chorus of the daughters of Ocean, and the appearance of Oceanus himself. The four elements occur frequently in *Moby-Dick*, one of those peculiarly American books in which almost everything takes place outdoors.

But there is another sense in which it is worth while considering the *Prometheus* in relation to *Moby-Dick*, and this is in the matter of the heroes. Aeschylus' Titan exists in a curious limbo between the mortal and the divine. Older, belonging to the race of divinities that preceded the Olympians, he is at the same time allied with the newer race of mankind. By his very existence he suggests an alternative world order. He is a figure of power; his suffering is in no way pathetic or pessimistic, but rather seems to hone and prepare him for a future liberation. If Ahab were simply a monomaniac piloting a ship and crew to disaster, he would be unimpressive as a hero because he would not suffer. If he were only human, on the other hand, his power over others would not be as hypnotic and mysterious as it is. In a certain sense, the Titan is a convincing type of the tragic hero, since he carries the essential notions of 1) re-ordering the cosmos according to an alternative plan, and 2) being at the same time divine and out of power. For if a hero is entirely single-minded, there is no occasion for a choice. Orestes could never turn to Pylades to ask advice before killing Clytemnestra, nor could Ahab be stricken with the recollection of home just before the third and final day of the chase.

The parallel, though interesting, is not immediately useful for the study of *Moby-Dick* in the tragic tradition, nor does the *Oresteia* seem close to Melville's mind. If, however, we examine the book's language and rhetoric, one additional point may be useful. I spoke previously of the tendency of tragedies to begin *in extremis*. *Moby-Dick* provides an example of this phenomenon. It begins at the edge of the world, the seacoast. But the extremism of the first paragraphs goes beyond this obvious fact. First, Ishmael tells us that he has "little or no money in my purse"; it is the extreme of the soul's season, "a damp, drizzly November in my soul." He finds himself "involuntarily pausing before coffin warehouses, and bringing up the rear of every funeral I meet." With this feeling of the end of life, he walks in New York down to the Battery, "its extreme down-town." To the crowd gathered by the wharfs he silently says, "Nothing will content them but the extremest limit of the land" (p. 12).

In *Kohlhaas*, this sense of crisis comes from the intrusion of disorder into a stable and orderly cosmos, and the language becomes highly wrought as if straining to deal with the tension. What then is unusual about the language of *Moby-Dick*? Sometimes, particularly in Ahab's soliloquies, it is clear that its source is Shakespeare. At other times it is a language of seafaring men, with all the special vocabulary involved in that profession, only transformed by the Quaker second person into a quasi-Biblical sonority. James Guetti, in *The Limits of Metaphor*, has enumerated the many specialized sets of terminology and concluded that "much of this book is composed of internally consistent and singularly limited verbal systems."[3] The reaction to the crisis takes the form of a continual donning and doffing of these vocabularies, so that, turning the page, the reader never knows whether to expect a philosophical discourse, a Shakespearean soliloquy, or a pseudoscientific ordering of cetological information. Behind this mixing of languages lies, of course, a mixing of ideologies, and with that realization we begin to close in on the tragic quality of the work. For just as Faulkner in *Absalom, Absalom!* will use a multiplicity of myths in order to avoid being enslaved by any single one of them, so Melville deals with vocabularies, and this is one of the reasons his book is puzzling to those who insist on a single generic name for what it is.

Still, the "crisis," as we have called it, is, at the start, limited to Ishmael's consciousness. This was certainly not true in Kleist, whatever influence Idealist philosophy may have had on his work. There the intrusion upon the order of Kohlhaas' world is as concrete and unavoidable as a tollgate. In *Moby-Dick*, the actual tragic conflict arises entirely from the human mind. For just as Ishmael's state of mental disorder at the start of the book is solely a result of his own longing for the sea, so too there

---

[3] James Guetti, *The Limits of Metaphor*, Ithaca, 1967, p. 16.

is no reason to think that the voyage of the *Pequod* would have been other than routine had not the obsession of its captain steered it relentlessly towards the capture of the white whale. At least, this is the way it seems—the quest of Ahab as the aggrandizement and concretion of the vaguer quest of Ishmael—until the third day of the chase, when Ahab suddenly says, "Aye, he's chasing *me* now; not I *him*—that's bad; I might have known it, too" (p. 461). Just as Kohlhaas becomes a greater intrusion upon the order of the world than was the tollgate that provoked him, so too, in the world of the *Pequod*, it is not long before we see that the white whale is no aberration at all compared with Ahab. In time, the close embrace of the doomed man and the factors that doom him is apparent in each of the two books. The absolutism of both works, like the onset of a dread disease, takes time to materialize.

It is necessary at this point to ascertain the nature of Ahab's absolutism, in what way it constitutes a disorder, and in what manner the disorder is finally resolved. Matthiessen and Olson remind us, first of all, that whaling was at the time one of the central industries of the young nation. Its exoticism would have been about as great as that of the airline business today, that is, dangerous and exciting but still essentially familiar. Unlike most present-day adventurers, however, the members of whaling crews were singularly underpaid, underfed and overworked. By the end of the eighteenth century, as Melville explains in *Billy Budd*, the exploitative conditions in conjunction with the necessarily crowded quarters kept the idea of mutiny alive in the sailors' minds. The order of the whal-

ers' microcosm was unstable to begin with. Without approaching the overbearing tyranny of an Ahab, an over-
zealous captain could turn any voyage into a floating hell.
In any case, the ship is best understood as an order of
production, a hierarchical enterprise conceived and exe-
cuted in the hope of material gain. Peleg and Bildad illustrate its laws: the minimization of costs and the maxi-
mization of profit. As in a modern piecework system, each
hand is paid according to the percentage of the final gross
of the voyage. It was therefore in the interest of every
officer and crewman alike to procure as many whales as
possible, thus creating an illusory sense of common enterprise among even the worst-paid seamen, or so at least the
owners must have hoped. Kleist referred the chronological setting of *Kohlhaas* to a time when middle-class enterprise was genuinely an individual effort, where one
man would raise horses and set off across the countryside
to sell them and do the best he could. Melville, however,
is speaking of a later stage in economic evolution, when,
in the name of individual or small-group ownership,
masses of other, non-owning people were employed to do
the actual task from which the owner was profiting. The
world of the whaling-ships may then be described in the
following terms. First, it was materialistic, not only in
the sense of that term that is opposed to spiritual, but
also in the sense that it is opposed to idealistic. Second,
it was a microcosm if anything more hierarchical than
the contemporary macrocosm in terms of duties and
compensation for those duties.

To begin with, Ahab intrudes upon the immediate
commercial object of the order, the procuring of whales.
His individual quest, in so far as it leads the ship away

from the customary areas of search and capture, is damaging not only to the owners of the craft but likewise to all of the members of the crew. If no whales are taken, there will be less money in the final "lay" or allotment for each man. Thus Starbuck answers Ahab in "The Quarter Deck": "I am game for the crooked jaw, and for the jaws of Death too, Captain Ahab, if it fairly comes in the way of the business we follow; but I came here to hunt whales, not my commander's vengeance. How many barrels will thy vengeance yield thee even if thou gettest it, Captain Ahab? It will not fetch thee much in our Nantucket market" (p. 143). By rights, such a rebellion against Ahab's purpose should have universal support; but it does not. One of the most savory ironies of the book is the way in which Ahab wins his men away from material interest in the journey—for he does it with the aid of a material incentive.

This is the gold doubloon which he nails to the mast, and which is to be the reward for the first man to spot the white whale. In one sense, it is true, this seems to be just an alternative material reward to the one offered by the company. It becomes, however, the vortex of the sort of anti-materialism that Ahab must propound to accomplish his purpose. "If money's to be the measurer, man, and the accountants have computed their great countinghouse the globe, by girdling it with guineas, one to every three parts of an inch; then, let me tell thee, that my vengeance will fetch a great premium here!" he says, striking his chest (pp. 143-144). But in the very same passage he repudiates the other, philosophical form of materialism, and opens a new complexity that momentarily takes the book beyond itself.

All visible objects, man, are but as pasteboard masks. But in each event—in the living act, the undoubted deed—there, some unknown but still reasoning thing puts forth the mouldings of its features from behind the unreasoning mask. If man will strike, strike through the mask! How can the prisoner reach outside except by thrusting through the wall? To me, the white whale is that wall, shoved near to me. Sometimes I think there's naught beyond. But 'tis enough. . . . That inscrutable thing is chiefly what I hate . . . (p. 144).

If we take this passage on a superficial level, it will appear to be a summary of that loose thread in the Kantian system, the *noumenon*. For although Kant set out to give certainty about perceptions by locating mechanisms for valid judgment of experience in every living mind, still he was unable to dispense with the concept of a necessarily unknowable substratum of all matter, a thing-in-itself that is somehow—we can never know how—responsible for the perceptions we receive, process, and validify. It was this same loose thread that was responsible for Kleist's "Kantian crisis" of 1801. Yet on closer examination it is clear that there is something larger operating here. Melville has made the *ding-an-sich* reasoning, and the phenomenon but an "unreasoning mask." There is an eerie proposition, reminiscent of Nerval's "Vers dorés," in which each material object conceals a living soul. For to make this substratum of matter sentient removes the problem from the realm of metaphysics pure and simple and complicates it with theology. What form might this reasoning *noumenon* take? And if it is at the foundation of all perception and judgment, why does it strike Ahab as hateful and evil? Why does he say, "be the white whale agent, or be the white whale principal, I will wreak that hate upon him" (p. 144).

A revealing passage is found in the chapter called "The Sermon," in the reflections on Jonah.

> Screwed at its axis against the side, a swinging lamp slightly oscillates in Jonah's room; and the ship, heeling over towards the wharf with the weight of the last bales received, the lamp, flame and all, though in slight motion, still maintains a permanent obliquity with reference to the room; though, in truth, infallibly straight itself, it but made obvious the false, lying levels among which it hung. The lamp alarms and frightens Jonah; as lying in his berth his tormented eyes roll around the place, and this thus far successful fugitive finds no refuge for his restless glance. But that contradiction in the lamp more and more appals him. The floor, the ceiling, and the side, are all awry. "Oh, so my conscience hangs in me!" he groans, "straight upward, so it burns; but the chambers of my soul are all in crookedness!" (p. 47).

In Melville there is frequently a tension between the relative, human world and the absolute, transcendent one. In *Pierre* the tension appears again in the tract on "Chronometricals and Horologicals," where it refers to temporality. Here, however, it is related to ethics, and we can see how this applies immediately to Ahab. A tragic hero is often in some sense alien, a figure who seems to come from far away. Ahab, "a grand, ungodly, god-like man" (p. 76), like Kohlhaas discards his domestic, ordinary life when his higher plan is conceived. We learn that "he has a wife—not three voyages wedded—a sweet, resigned girl. Think of that; by that sweet girl that old man has a child" (p. 77). Yet he never mentions them until the very end, among omens of doom, when the full force of choice comes upon him: "Close! Stand close to me, Starbuck; let me look into a human eye; it is better than to gaze into sea or sky; better than to gaze upon God. . . . I see my wife and child in thine eye" (p. 444). Just as Jonah in his berth is tortured, vertiginous from knowledge of the upright, absolute flame, so that the human world seems askew by comparison, so too Ahab has seen something as absolute as God and cannot return from that vision to ordinary existence. Even when the choice—Achilles' choice—presents itself so explicitly, the vision of the absolute is so ingrained in the hero that he cannot conceive of it as an actual decision. "Fate" is simply a matter of being true to one's own nature. It is not the action of free will, nor the reaction of necessity, but rather the elusive middle-ground of enaction. The tragic hero lives by the upright flame while the remainder of mankind live by the floor, the ceiling and the walls. He is, as Hegel saw, the delegate of the absolute. Forever lonely, he can say, "Ahab stands alone among the millions of the peopled earth, nor gods nor men his neighbors" (p. 452). In moments of apparent detachment he may admit to being mad, or may question in sudden terror who he is and what terror has come into him to make him so. "Is Ahab, Ahab?" he may ask, "Is it I, God, or who, that lifts this arm?" (p. 445).

Like the flame, Ahab chooses his direction on a universal and absolute basis in the midst of a world content with relative good. Rather, this direction will choose him, and this is the significance of the previous encounter between the captain and the white whale. The snapped leg is like the wound through which the serpent injected his poison. It is like the murder of Kohlhaas' wife. It is the point of no return. But, allowing this absolute commitment in Ahab, what then is the nature of the absolute? With Kleist, it was a matter of an abstraction's—Justice's —acquiring transcendental meaning, becoming an inviolable category. In Melville, however, the *noumenon* is possibly gifted with reason, as we saw before. We will pierce through the mask, find perhaps nothing, perhaps the thing-in-itself, perhaps a sentient, causal being. We are led to believe that this is the standard of transcendental truth, like the flame, even though Ishmael sees in the Leviathan "a colorless, all-color of atheism" (p. 169). If, however, the whale is meant to embody that kind of absolute, we must still explain the constant associations of evil and death, unless we are content to attribute these to the same dreadful vertigo felt by Jonah watching the world become meaningless in the light of his insight.

Since we could assign no motive to Kohlhaas' choice of death over life—save that, having tasted the absolute, having committed himself as Achilles did, he could never again return to the life of the family and seasons—we chose then to assign to the capsule he wears around his neck the meaning of absoluteness itself, condensed and essential. Likewise, to assign a single meaning to the whale detracts from its immensity and scales down the far-reaching implications of the tragedy. We can only decide that the significance of the whale is significance itself It is heartless significance; it leaves us living with "half a heart." It is what D. H. Lawrence called "a truth that kills." It is not the meaning that love gives us, nor even the diabolism of genuine hatred. What is so poisonous and evil about the emblem is that it stands for the most intellectual sort of meaning. It is an Apollonian goal of perfection, the axis toward which the parabola forever moves without touching. It is tyrannical Mind tirelessly and destructively searching for its own reflection in the material objects of the world.

"Chance, free will, and necessity—no wise incompatible—all interweavingly working together" (p. 185). So Ishmael, in "The Mat-Maker," summarizes in a sentence the solution to that age-old problem of tragedy. And Ahab, as he says, is forever Ahab. It is his essential nature to be purely Mind, and to protest against the exigencies of the body that his fierce quest is already destroying. "Gifted with the high perception, I lack the low, enjoying power" (p. 147), he says of himself in a soliloquy. Cursing the carpenter who makes his ivory leg, a man he calls Prometheus, Ahab turns on the body: "By heavens! I'll get a crucible, and into it, and dissolve myself down to one small, compendious vertebra. So" (p. 392). In "The Pipe," he discards that humble instrument of pleasure, his language of rejection again recalling that of Achilles: "What business have I with this pipe? This thing that is meant for sereneness, to send up mild white vapors among mild white hairs, not among torn iron-gray locks like mine. I'll smoke no more—" (p. 114). Even such mundane incidents in *Moby-Dick* are crowned with a grandeur by virtue of the language of the book. With its huge rhetorical democracy, it shows that tragedy is not only a function of titular nobility and vast political gesture. We should not hesitate to apply to passages like these the phrase of Nietzsche that has so much to do with Ahab: "Apollo's majestic rejection of all license."[4]

The other characters in the work set up different dialectical relationships with their captain, and they form a chorus each member of which embodies some aspect of the Dionysian. Sometimes, as in "Midnight, Forecastle," it may take the form of a choric revelry, the men dancing and singing far into the night, chanting the paean for the search of the white whale. "I, Ishmael," says the narrator, "was one of that crew" (p. 155). So is Starbuck, in his "mere unaided virtue of right-mindedness" (p. 162), who becomes at last a spokesman for the values of the shore, the home, the family, and all that Ahab has rejected. So too is Stubb, who stands against Ahab intellectually, saying, "Think not, is my eleventh commandment" (p. 114). Then there is Flask, who sees in the doubloon only the satisfaction of smaller pleasures. For him, the gold piece is "nine hundred and sixty cigars" (p. 361). But mainly it is Ishmael who stands in contrast to his captain, bipartite Ishmael, who, like Quentin in *Absalom, Absalom!*, is sometimes a character and sometimes, with visionary omniscience, a narrator. He is Horatio, the survivor charged with the obligation to tell the tale to others far from the actual event. But he is a Dionysian man, because he affirms the continuity and universality of life against a pathology of illusions.

His feeling for Queequeg is the only vital and candid affection in the book. He speaks with the same pride

[4] Friedrich Nietzsche, *The Birth of Tragedy and The Case of Wagner*, trans. Walter Kaufmann, New York, 1967, p. 26.

about the process of whaling and its harvest that any farmer out of Hesiod might show. Observant, sometimes sensuous, he does not feel compelled to justify something intellectually in order to glory in its full effect. Hence he can say about the whiteness of the whale that it is a "vague, nameless horror" which he must "almost despair of putting in comprehensible form" (p. 163). He over-uses the word "thing" throughout the book. Instead of seeking perfection, completeness, total knowledge as Ahab does, he says instead, "God keep me from ever completing anything" (p. 128).

But it is in the terrifying chapter called "The Try-Works" that his relation to Ahab becomes clear. Having night-duty at the tiller, Ishmael confronts the fires of the try-works, huge kilns where oil is extracted from the blubber of the whale by cooking at intense heat. While observing the commotion of harpooners and other crew-men around this fire, he has a sort of hell-vision, seeing the spectacle before him as "the material counterpart of her monomaniac commander's soul" (p. 354). This refers in part to the pact which Ahab is thought by some to have made, Faust-like, with the diabolical Fedallah, his har-pooner. Ishmael goes on: "Wrapped, for that interval, in darkness myself, I but better saw the redness, the mad-ness, the ghastliness of others" (p. 354). Here he is sim-ply reacting to Ahab with the terror of a reflective, re-active man at the sight of all that industry in the service of some great achievement, just as the old men in the *Agamemnon*, tired of war and longing for the restoration of order, react with horror at the bloody deeds they have to witness. Then Ishmael falls asleep: "I thought my eyes were open; I was half conscious of putting my fingers to the lids and mechanically stretching them still further apart." Here he is experiencing the consciousness of an Ahab, becoming for the moment an idealist like his captain. The seen phenomena are no longer important; perception becomes interior, categories of the mind operating back onto the mind itself. "But, spite of all this, I could see no compass before me to steer by. . . . Nothing seemed before me but a jet gloom, now and then made ghastly by flashes of redness. . . . A stark, bewildered feeling, as of death, came over me. Convulsively my hands grasped the tiller, but with the crazy conceit that the tiller was, somehow, in some enchanted way, inverted." What has happened, on the literal level, is that in his doze Ishmael has turned backward, facing the stern, so that he too is for the time inverted. If he did not awaken when he did, the ship might very well have capsized. But on another level what has happened is that an interiorization of experience has nearly proven fatal to external experience; the world of the mind and the self has barely missed capsizing reality. "Look not too long in the face of the fire, O man!" he warns, "Never dream with thy hand on the helm. Turn not thy back to the compass; accept the first hint of the hitching tiller; believe not the artificial fire. . . . Tomorrow, in the natural sun, the skies will be bright. . . ."

But Ishmael is not being facile and optimistic in rejecting the nightmare of Ahab's interior world. Like the choruses of the Greek stage, he will experience joy and woe with the same vitality, so long as they are real, and not of the world of fire, the Apollonian dream-world, as Nietzsche called it. Thus, he says, "the sun hides not Virginia's Dismal Swamp, nor Rome's accursed Campagna, nor wide Sahara, nor all the millions of miles of deserts and of griefs beneath the moon" (pp. 354-55). He will agree with Ecclesiastes that all is vanity. But he will not go chasing the artificial absolute fire of the intellect, nor any emblematic white whale. "Give not thyself up, then, to fire, lest it invert thee, deaden thee; as for the time it did me" (p. 354). This is the crux of the opposition between Ishmael and Ahab; yet we see that it is not so much an opposition as a complement, more in the nature of true dialectic, the sort that Nietzsche had in mind when he described the structure of ancient tragedy.

"And I only am escaped alone to tell thee." This is the epigraph that heads the final, dramatic epilogue that Ishmael speaks at the close of the book, when the disaster is consummated. At last we have come to the restoration of order, to that terrible silence after tragedy when "the sea rolled on as it rolled five thousand years ago" (p. 469). Ishmael only has ridden up out of the draw of the sinking ship, floating on the coffin made by his friend Queequeg. It is a blatant enough emblem of life triumphing over death, and it is moving enough, but it is not the only compensation that is given for the loss of the ship and the final disaster of Ahab's dream. Indeed, compensation is one of the continuing concerns of the tragedy as a whole, as it must be with all meaningful tragedies, lest they become what Schopenhauer said they ought to be —mere cautions against the undertaking of all endeavor.

There are two images of compensation in the work that I would take as central. The first is the metaphor of the Catskill eagle at the end of "The Try-Works."

And there is a Catskill eagle in some souls that can alike dive down into the blackest gorges, and soar out of them again and become invisible in the sunny spaces. And even if he for ever flies within the gorge, that gorge is in the mountains; so that even in his lowest swoop the mountain eagle is still higher than other birds upon the plain, even though they soar (p. 355).

Coming on the heels of the passage about the fire which we have examined, this does not refer to Ahab, who is a prey to the illusory flames, dead and inverted in spite of all his determination and grandeur. Here, Ishmael is talking instead about that emotive, compassionate end of tragedy of which he is the delegate in the novel. In some sense, it is a creed of the choric man, that he can experience the blackest depths and the greatest heights without artificiality; that he can experience all the extremism of tragedy and remain normative; and that his norm is intrinsically more elevated than that of the man who experiences less. Given the same choice that Achilles was given, Ishmael would opt for life, yet at the same time would not exchange a head-on glimpse of death for anything. Dionysos is the creature who embraces the coffin, the actuality of death, not as a life-negating power, but as an impetus to greater vitality. The heights to which we soar are meaningless unless there is a depth as well; mountains are defined only by the existence of their valleys. In this way we can understand, in the archetypal image of Ishmael rising from the waters of death and clinging to a coffin for his life, the notion of tragic compensation from the choric, from Ishmael's, point of view.

To understand how compensation operates in the case of the hero, Ahab, is another matter. For if there is a question of a moral, if there is any sort of punishment in the catastrophe of the work, then it is not tragic in any complete sense. There must be some endemic glory in a hero's action which balances and compensates his end. For Ahab, this force is partly verbal, just as it is for, say, Macbeth. In the splendor of his language, especially in the moments of clarity when he sees his monomania with the detachment of an outsider, there is nearly enough strength to counteract whatever ethical judgments may be made against him. But Melville does not let it stop at that. There is another passage that serves for Ahab a function similar to that which the Catskill eagle passage served for Ishmael. This is a moment that comes at the end of the book, when the ship is sinking and Ahab has already disappeared, strapped to the back of the submerging white whale that was his obsession:

But as the last whelmings intermixingly poured themselves over the sunken head of the Indian at the mainmast, leaving a few inches of the erect spar yet visible, together with long streaming yards of the flag, which calmly undulated, with ironical coincidings, over the destroying billows they almost touched;—at that instant, a red arm and a hammer hovered backwardly uplifted in the open air, in the act of nailing the flag faster and yet faster to the subsiding spar. A sky-hawk that tauntingly had followed the main-truck downwards from its natural home among the stars, pecking at the flag, and incommoding Tashtego there; his bird now chanced to intercept its broad fluttering wing between the hammer and the wood; and simultaneously feeling that etherial thrill, the submerged savage beneath, in his death-gasp, kept his hammer frozen there; and so the bird of heaven, with archangelic shrieks, and his imperial beak thrust upwards, and his whole captive form folded in the flag of Ahab, went down with his ship, which, like Satan, would not sink to hell till she had dragged a living part of heaven along with her, and helmeted herself with it (p. 469).

This scene is several things at once, all of them pertaining directly to the matter of tragic compensation. In the first place, it is necessary to accept the fact that the scene is unrealistic, although remotely possible. There are many places in the book about which this could be said, but this instance, coming as it does near the very end, is peculiarly emblematic. It is an oddly intellectual emblem, too, as is fitting for Ahab, except that it is charged with emotion by virtue of its position in the closing chapter. Here again the image is a bird, only not a mountain eagle who moves among peaks and depressions, but a sea-hawk whose elevation is constant. We are told, however, that his home is among the stars. He is "archangelic" and "imperial," haughty, distant, and alone—in short, a bird fit to be folded in the flag of Ahab. This alien bird is possessed to come down and touch the sinking ship, just as lonely obsession with knowledge made Ahab seem distant and alien from the world. Ahab and the bird are crucified in different ways, Ahab with rope to the back of Moby-Dick, the bird with nails onto the crossed mast. Tashtego, below, feels an "etherial thrill" at catching life with his hammer; the event is at once a killing and an affirmative clutching at living. This embrace is the equivalent for Ahab of Ishmael's embrace of the coffin. It is not only a compensation, as the text tells us, for all the death and hell, caught in a piece of life and heaven; but it is also emblematic of the fact that although Ahab is dead, that although his desire for superhuman knowledge has placed him past the human state in death, he like the bird is still at the apex of the world, although that world is sinking to the deep; that within the limited possibilities of actual knowing, he exceeded all others while still remaining thankfully mortal. Like Achilles, like the sky-hawk, Ahab is cut off, imperfect, but forever trying to move upward, to surpass the limits. The disorder and death he made in the world, with his absolutism, his inhuman, celestial time, is justified in the sinews of that bird. From its home among the stars, it goes to the depths. But, unlike Ishmael's Catskill eagle, it has no norm between, it can never exist on the mere plane of things, on a mere surface, in the good anonymity in which less damned creatures, and less fortunate ones, live to their ripe old age.

4 *Toward Lyric Tragedy: W. B. Yeats*

Among the members of the Rhymers' Club, to which Yeats belonged, was Ernest Dowson, who wrote the following poem:

They are not long, the weeping and the laughter,
　Love and desire and hate:
I think they have no portion with us after
　We pass the gate.

They are not long, the days of wine and roses:
　Out of a misty dream
Our path emerges for a while, then closes
　Within a dream.

Here, encapsulated, is the transcendental aestheticism that makes the "action" of a contemporary play, such as Swinburne's *Atalanta*, or narrative poem, such as Mallarmé's *Hérodiade*, so static and listless. There is no confrontation whose stakes involve the emotional and spiritual cartography of an entire new world. Instead, this is the poetry of a flagging civilization or, at any rate, one that suspected its days of ascendancy were over. It is poetry without a future, and with an overbearing past. Any dramatic action that could be devised would only remind someone of a previous play, any ideology one might incorporate into verse had already been fully developed elsewhere. Yeats' early poetry—for example "The Lake

Isle of Innisfree," "The Song of Wandering Aengus" or the Rose poems—partakes of this lethargy. Strangely enough, even at the height of his public career in the Abbey Theatre, Yeats never really produced a play of action. Even the partisan women, fashioned out of his image of Maud Gonne, are still a little close to the heavy-eyed damozels of Rossetti paintings. In an unsatisfying essay called "The Tragic Theatre," he speaks of Synge's Deirdre in "a reverie of passion that mounts and mounts till grief itself has carried her beyond grief into pure contemplation."[1] In *The Trembling of the Veil*, he recalls his youth as being "in all things pre-Raphaelite,"[2] and some of the passivity implied in the assertion remains throughout even the most mature work.

"The Tragic Theatre" dates from 1910, when Yeats' dissatisfaction with his own work was strongest. "I could find," he wrote, "nothing to make a song about but kings, / Helmets, and swords, and half-forgotten things. . . ." In "The Fascination of What's Difficult," he laid his "curse on plays / That have to be set up in fifty ways, / On the day's war with every knave and dolt, / Theatre business, management of men." Having run aestheticism and the poetic thinking of the Rhymers' Club to an end, Yeats plunged into the highly political world of Irish theatre. Yet even in his role as a public man, he was never able fully to shake the pre-Raphaelite belief in a pure, uninvolved, and static beauty. This was certainly the role in which his mind had cast Maud Gonne, before he discovered she was a woman of action. Here, in the first

[1] W. B. Yeats, *Essays and Introductions*, New York, 1968, p. 239.
[2] W. B. Yeats, *Autobiography*, New York, 1938, p. 100.

of his youth, began the dialectic that would in time lead him to tragedy.

In Yeats' case the application of dialectical notions of tragedy is not an abstract problem. We know that he began reading Nietzsche in 1902,[3] and although it is not certain which works he read, it seems likely that *Die Geburt der Tragödie* would have attracted him. Certain passages in "The Tragic Theatre" seem to support that possibility. There is, for example, a discussion of the "antithesis between character and lyric poetry," which is a restatement of the Apollonian/stage versus Dionysian/chorus distinction in Nietzsche's work (*Essays*, p. 240). *A Vision* as well is a profoundly dialectical construct, so much so that parts of it bear the stamp of Hegel, although Yeats protests that the spirits that dictated its content asked him not to read any philosophy until it was completed.[4] Nevertheless, the written work as we have it—of course it comes much later than the visions themselves—mentions Hegel's *Logic* several times, and on one occasion actually quotes from it at length (*A Vision*, p. 249).

Every tragic writer has his own version of the tragic dialectic. Any of these versions can be seen in general terms as an intrusion of one order upon another, incompatible one. In Kleist, we saw the absolutism of Kohlhaas intruding upon the bourgeois world with its sanctity of family, negotiation and compromise. In Melville, we saw Ahab, obsessed with the *noumenon* of absolute knowledge, imposing a single monomaniacal and alien enter-

[3] W. B. Yeats, *Eleven Plays*, ed. A. Norman Jeffares, New York, 1964, introduction by Jeffares, p. 4.
[4] W. B. Yeats, *A Vision*, New York, 1956, p. 12.

prise upon the commercial venture of the *Pequod*. Yeats' version, though, changes and develops throughout his career. In *The Countess Cathleen* of 1892, it is a brilliant attack on the problem of Christian tragedy, in which a thoroughly Christian action on the part of the protagonist paradoxically brings her into conflict with Christian doctrine in a manner that should damn her. At this early stage, however, the poet is unwilling to relinquish his countess, who is clearly modeled on Maud Gonne. Therefore she is saved by a classical *deus ex machina*, and an angel appears to reassure her poet-lover Aleel that she has been admitted into Heaven. Another early play, *The Land of Heart's Desire*, also deals with a conflict of two orders, the faery realm intruding upon conventional Irish society, and the conflict is resolved only when Mary, the character within whom the opposition is focused, dies into the faery world. Yet although it is possible to recognize the basic form of tragic action in the piece, it is difficult to see the necessity of the opposition. That is to say, the intrusion of imagination into the quotidian world is not necessarily catastrophic, and the play is not strong enough to convince us that it is. And yet, even within this marked pre-Raphaelite beginning, the seeds of Yeats' later and more sophisticated notions of tragedy are securely planted.

The dialectic defined in the early work is between, say, "The Lake Isle of Innisfree" in 1893 and *Cathleen Ni Houlihan* of 1902, and may be described without great oversimplification as a conflict of withdrawal, contemplation and re-action on the one hand, and involvement and action on the other. This of course would have made Yeats highly susceptible to a reading of *The Birth of Tragedy*, which elaborates abstractions of that sort into mythic complexes, into modes of consciousness. For although it is generally thought that all of Yeats' notions about tragedy derive either from his practical experience at the Abbey Theatre, or else from the content of *A Vision*, it seems to me that this distinction is artificial, in the first place, and that in the second place neither aspect should be separated from theoretical material to which he was exposed. In addition, Helen Vendler has demonstrated that many of the concepts that are central to *A Vision* appear earlier in Yeats' writing than does the automatic writing and his notes on it, which begin in 1917.[5] The transition from early, naive oppositions of faeries and Irish revolutionaries to later sophistications is quite continuous all through the period of political and theatrical involvement, and indeed the revelations of *A Vision*, and what it teaches us about tragedy, follow quite naturally even from this earlier period.

Let us consider, for example, the play of 1908 known as *The Unicorn from the Stars*, a revision of an earlier piece called *Where There Is Nothing*. This play bears some resemblance to previous works such as *The Land of Heart's Desire*, in that one of the characters is given a transcendental capacity which proves to be his undoing. In *The Unicorn from the Stars*, however, the transcendence is much more potent than a kingdom of faeries, and the society against which it brings its disorder is better defined in terms of, once again, trade and economics. The Hearnes are a family of coachbuilders, and the eldest, Thomas, is a solid, commercial man who

[5] Helen Vendler, *Yeats' Vision and the Later Plays*, Cambridge, Mass., 1963, p. 13.

believes that "a dream is a sort of a shadow, no profit in it to any one at all."[6] He has a nephew, Martin, who is in the business, and who is subject to prolonged states of trance. In the opening lines, a priest has come to see Martin, who is in the grip of the most serious trance of his life. With the sense of extreme that often accompanies the onset of tragedy, the priest says after examining the young man that "it is either the best thing or the worst thing that can happen to anyone, that is happening to him now" (*Plays*, p. 215). As a bourgeois craftsman with a stake in the preservation of order, Thomas fears that the spells will somehow drive his nephew "against the Government maybe the same as Johnny Gibbons that is at this time an outlaw" (*Plays*, p. 216). In other words, he sees transcendence as a legal threat, just the way the Elector conceives of Kohlhaas.

When Martin awakens, Father John asks him what he saw. He answers, "Do you not smell the broken fruit —the grapes? The room is full of the smell. . . . There were horses—white horses rushing by, with white shining riders—there was a horse without a rider, and some one caught me up and put me on him and we rode away, with the wind, like the wind" (*Plays*, p. 219). These horses are certainly related to those described in the poet's note to "Nineteen Hundred and Nineteen": "The countrypeople see at times certain apparitions whom they name now 'fallen angels,' now 'ancient inhabitants of the country,' and describe as riding at whiles 'with flowers upon the heads of the horses.' "[7] These, along with the Dionysian emblem of the grapes are delegates from an-

---

6 W. B. Yeats, *Collected Plays*, New York, 1953, p. 213.

7 W. B. Yeats, *Collected Poems*, New York, 1950, p. 455.

other world, a world that will later be identified by
Yeats with the future, the coming of the next gyre. But
at this time it is best glossed by the refrain from a 1904
poem called "The Withering of the Boughs," which
reads:

> No boughs have withered because of the wintry wind;
> The boughs have withered because I have told them
>   my dreams (*Poems*, p. 77).

Against the neatly ordered domain of craftsmen, of me-
thodical makers, Martin's vision is a dream of primal
strength, pure or, as Father John says, "virginal strength,"
an energy that will wither the actual world with its sur-
den fury. Thomas, like a wounded and disillusioned parent, bemoans the young man's resistance to his discipline.
His own brother, Andrew, used to have similar visions
until Thomas "cured" him, "taking you in hand and
binding you to the hours of the clock" (*Plays*, p. 221).
Martin says of Thomas that "He has never heard the
laughter and the music beyond" (*Plays*, p. 223).

But what is beyond is much more serious than only
laughter and music. Martin continues to try to recall
the remainder of his vision that his sudden awakening by
Father John has temporarily driven from his mind. "I
saw," he says, "a bright many-changing figure; it was
holding up a shining vessel; then the vessel fell and was
broken with a great crash; then I saw the unicorns tram-
pling it. They were breaking the world to pieces—when
I saw the cracks coming I shouted for joy! And I heard
the command, 'Destroy, destroy, destruction is the life-
giver! Destroy!'" (*Plays*, p. 225). Here is the most striking precursor of the 'tragic joy' of *Last Poems*, the asser-

tion that "Hamlet and Lear are gay" (*Poems*, p. 292). For in 1908, nine years before the first spiritual manifestation, there is already an implicit association of the ideas of destruction and rebuilding. "To destroy, to overthrow all that comes between us and God, between us and that shining country" (*Plays*, p. 225). This is reminiscent of Melville's caution against men who operate according to some absolute.

The poor, who in *The Unicorn from the Stars* are represented by a troop of errant beggars, become a kind of chorus for the actions undertaken by Martin: "The poor, they have nothing, and so they can see Heaven as we cannot" (*Plays*, p. 225). In the second act, Martin lures a group of these beggars to his house with drink and food, and tries to organize them into an army of destruction.

> Martin: I saw the unicorns trampling in my dream. They were breaking the world. I am to destroy; destruction was the word the messenger spoke.
> Father John: To destroy?
> Martin: To bring again the old disturbed exalted life, the old splendour (*Plays*, pp. 226-227).

And so, like other tragic heroes, Martin is confronted with the traditional choice. Father John, deploring the passage of that exaltation, says, "Men were holy then, there were saints everywhere. There was reverence; but now it is all work, business, how to live a long time" (*Plays*, p. 227). Martin opts for seizing the moment at hand. "Why should we be patient? To live seventy years, and others to come after us and live seventy years, it may be; and so from age to age, and all the while the old splendour dying more and more" (*Plays*, p. 227).

And so once again there is an opposition of the world of work, family, profit, and longevity with a dangerous and armed delegate from an absolute realm. "We will get no help from settled men," says Martin, "we will call to the lawbreakers, the tinkers, the sievemakers, the sheep-stealers" (*Plays*, p. 230). Soon the whole countryside, in a kind of epidemic, is no longer working, but gathers at various points to drink and carouse. After more pro-nouncements against the law, Martin, like Kohlhaas, an-nounces his army: "We will go out against the world and break it and unmake it. We are the army of the Uni-corn from the Stars!" (*Plays*, p. 233). And this is what they will fight for, their vision of paradise: "Their days were a dance bred of the secret frenzy of their hearts, or a battle where the sword made a sound that was like laughter" (*Plays*, p. 234). For Martin, paradise is a world where a genuine communality exists, where the heart governs action directly, and where symbols of Apol-lonian striving, like the sword, are turned to immediate examples of human emotion, like laughter.

In the third act, however, when the night of destruc-tion is done with, Martin falls into another trance in which he sees that he has misjudged his vision of the previous day. The curious inversion of his revelation makes the ending of the play very puzzling. He discovers from the second vision that his "business is not reforma-tion but revelation," and that "the battle that we have to fight is fought out in our own mind" (*Plays*, p. 243). Heaven is re-envisioned as a place whose music "is made of the continual clashing of swords!" (*Plays*, p. 242). Here "the lover still loves, but with a greater passion, and the rider still rides, but the horse goes like the wind and leaps the ridges, and the battle goes on, always, always. That is the joy of Heaven, continual battle" (*Plays*, p. 245). At the same time, access to that Heaven is not through action on earth, but in a sort of Schopenhauerian suppression of the senses—"where there is nothing— there is God!" (*Plays*, p. 245). So that instead of having to destroy the old civilization to let loose the fury, now it is necessary to sink into oblivion and find that fury in the beyond. In one sense, this is something of an anticlimax, since the new vision is less energetic than its predecessor. When the constable shoots Martin just after he has articulated this new revelation, the young man is no longer a threat to the order of work and family. Yet— in another reversal—at the end he imagines himself climbing toward Paradise, only now he does not mention continual battle, but reverts to talk of "the vineyards of Eden" (*Plays*, p. 246), suggesting the earlier Dionysianism. As in *The Countess Cathleen*, a flawed ending prevents actual tragedy. Yet again the tragic elements are clear—a major step in Yeats' development, since neither of the two orders in conflict is a realm of nostalgic beauty, of faeries. Now the two poles of the conflict are both tenable in the world.

With the advent of his wife's automatic writing in 1917—or, more accurately, somewhat before that, as we will see—Yeats' notion of tragedy changed in accordance with the tenets of his prophetic book. Suddenly order and disorder are no longer personal or national issues. If they are to be significant, they must partake directly of the Absolute, rechristened Spiritus Mundi. The main difference between Yeats and the dialectical philosophers whom he is obviously following—Hegel, for example—

is that *A Vision* is just what its title says it is. It has no pretensions to science. Where Hegel derives all the phenomena of the world through a series of logical syllogisms, Yeats relies on the power of revelation, although he is not averse to charts and diagrams, the equipment that is the fascination and the bane of all occultism. With Blake, he seems to have believed that much of his writing was "dictated" from beyond. In any case, it is clear that the dialectical nature of his system is in some sense or another related to the dialectical nature of tragedy, to which he was led more and more insistently as he aged.

For this reason, it is necessary that we come to some understanding of that system, even though much of it is obscure and does not yield well to even the most diligent study.

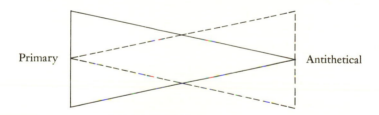

In this familiar diagram, the growth of one opposite is seen as inversely proportional to the other's. Like the ends of a see-saw, one pole of the dialectic can ascend only as the other declines. If we call the gyre in solid lines the *primary*, we can see that it can expand only as the broken-lined or *antithetical* gyre diminishes, and vice-versa. All dialectics in Yeats' poetry of the period are derived from this abstract mechanism, and the diagram of the phases of the moon comes directly from it

as well. Thus, where Hegelian dialectics are progres-
sive, with so many syllogisms back to back leading to
increasing knowledge of the world, Yeatsian dialectics
are cyclic, so that there is never anything new under the
sun except in the sense that spring is "new" after winter.
Like any cycle, Yeats' is divided into phases: first into
halves—its ascendant and descendent; then into quarters
—progression toward strength, exercise of strength, waning of strength, and loss of strength, and then into
twenty-eight specific phases corresponding to the phases
of the moon, each with its own distinct character. From
these is drawn the circular diagram of which the following is a simplification.

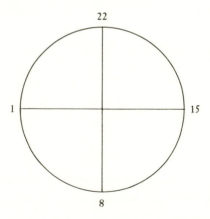

This sort of chart is not unusual in occult systems, and
its uniqueness in Yeats is only that it is derived wholly
from the gyres, so that the theory of personality is directly related to, say, the theory of history. The circle
is intended to be a two-dimensional metaphor for the
same thing for which the gyre is a three-dimensional

metaphor. Hence the character of every phase is determined not only by its own position in the circle, but also by its diagonal opposite and the "mirror image" of the diagonal. For example, phase 17 is affected by phase 3 and phase 27. In addition, a personality of any phase may be "in phase" or "out of phase." This ambivalence is found in the reading of the Tarot deck, and even in orthodox medieval allegory. Thus a person of the early phases may be a pure and natural man, or else he may absorb some quality of the late phases and become a "natural" in the sense of a fool.

Yet the major dialectic of the wheel and thus of the gyres as well is the distinction called "primary-antithetical" as defined by the valences of the two "impossible" phases, 1 and 15. These are impossible since they are pure and hence inhuman, the first being absolute objectivity, and the fifteenth pure subjectivity. It is at this point that the exact relationship of *A Vision* to *The Birth of Tragedy* can be ascertained. The primary phases are those approaching or recently departed from phase 15. "When the old antithetical becomes the new primary," he writes, "moral feeling is changed into an organisation of experience which must in its turn seek a unity, the whole of experience. When the old primary becomes the new antithetical, the old realisation of an objective moral law is changed into a subconscious turbulent instinct. The world of rigid custom and law is broken up by 'the uncontrollable mystery upon the bestial floor' " (*A Vision*, p. 105). Here we see an apparent similarity to the Nietzschean dialectic, not as it was altered for the purposes of this study in the first chapter, but in its original form. The characteristic of phase 1 we are told, is "perfect plasticity," which should recall the identification of the Apollonian with the plastic arts, especially with the figures on the Parthenon. So too the figures associated with that gyre, the primary, have as their goal *unity*, which is the same as the concept of *individuation* in *The Birth of Tragedy*. Phase 15, at the center of the antithetical gyre, is characterized by "pure beauty," the lyric, the subjective and re-active, the choric. Unlike Nietzsche, Yeats does not give either of the gyres the generative quality that the Dionysian has. Instead, they exist in a cyclical alternation, and it is this alternation that runs through several paired sets of Yeats' poems, the ones leading most directly to the full development of an idea of tragedy in the *Last Poems*.

As Yeats grows older, his concern becomes increasingly apocalyptic. The beginning of the next gyre, which is constantly foreshadowed in our time, may be best described as a Dionysian event. Yet although we experience strong and terrifying premonitions of the next gyre, we still belong to the present one, which is to say that we still require customs, laws, and forms of order to survive. So we witness politicians calling for law and order in vain, while Dionysos day by day converts new followers in all areas of life. Joseph Frank has suggested that tragedy arises soon after the collapse of formal religion as an organizing principle in society, but before the old categories of that creed have wholly lapsed. Here we think less of Aeschylus than of Shakespeare writing at the end of Medieval Christianity, or of Yeats writing in what he doubtless felt to be the end of Irish Catholicism. Under these circumstances, people are compelled to make religious, ethical and political decisions without having any automatic means for arriving at a conclusion. This opens the possibility of error at the same time that it raises the perhaps illusory ideal of a new glory. Hence, instead of being content with standing structures and the normal heights which they allow men safely to reach, men tend to reach for greater heights on less secure scaffolding. It is possible to accept Yeats' belief in his own system at those moments when he is pleading for greater expansiveness of heart, courtesy, and compassion in the face of the rising storm. And yet, in view of the inevitability of the cataclysm, it does not seem that there can be any genuine tragic heroism in the conventional sense. Martin in *The Unicorn from the Stars* is a man more of prophecy than of action. We may attribute this characteristic to the early pre-Raphaelite associations, with all the stasis and passivity of this school. Yet this proposition, though partly right, does not entirely explain that lack which the poet tried—anachronistically—to eliminate in his Cuchulain plays and in his versions of Sophocles. For as his preoccupation with tragedy grew, his dramas became more and more symbolic, more and more ritualistic and shimmering with the cold thrill of the supernatural. "No man has ever prayed to or dreaded one of Vergil's nymphs, but when Oedipus at Colonus went into the Wood of the Furies he felt the same creeping in his flesh that an Irish countryman feels in certain haunted woods in Galway and in Sligo."

These words appeared in a notice Yeats gave to the *New York Times* of January 15, 1933.[8] In the same piece, he defines the aim of his project as the production of "a

[8] Reprinted in W. B. Yeats, *Collected Letters*, ed. Allen Wade, London, 1954, p. 537.

plain man's Oedipus." He describes the enthusiastic reception of *Oedipus the King* at the Abbey Theatre in 1926, and attributes this to the fact that "I may not have gone to Greece through a Latin mist. Greek literature, like old Irish literature, was founded upon belief, not like Latin literature upon documents." In the *Oedipus* he found a hero who resembled the Irish Cuchulain of national myth. As seen in the *Tain Bo Cualnge*, Cuchulain is a Protean figure, sometimes purely heroic, sometimes comic, sometimes enduring loss. As John X.W.P. Corcoran wrote, "Although invincible he was not invulnerable and his body was sorely wounded on a number of occasions. To the Celts their hero had to suffer as a mortal else he would have been lessened in their eyes."[9] The sufferings of Oedipus clearly qualify him as human enough for an audience accustomed to that most immediate form of heroism. Yet, not really paradoxically, in a letter to Olivia Shakespear on the eve of the first performance of the play, December 7, 1926, Yeats affirms "a sense as of the actual presence in a terrible sacrament of the god" (*Letters*, p. 720).

Oedipus shares with Cuchulain more than a capacity for suffering. Like the legendary Celt, he embodies certain aspects of the self-regard of the race. If Cuchulain's range is broad, so is Oedipus', who is first king, then suppliant, then near divine. Oedipus covers a correspondingly broad geographical area, reigning in Thebes and coming to die in Athens. Embracing the synthesis born of the *Oresteia*, he comes to the grove of the Furies in Colonus and asks grace not only for himself but for Apol-

[9] "Celtic Mythology," *New Larousse Encyclopedia of Mythology*, New York, 1968, p. 233.

lo. Although the two plays Yeats translated are not part of the same trilogy, one cannot help but feel a continuity. For in the *Tyrannos* his relentless thirst for truth shattered the apparent order and revealed a new and terrible one that ruined him. In the *Coloneus* he has suffered and grown sufficiently to approach the precinct of the Eumenides, who have become the spirits of home, whose domain he has above all others violated. In the redemptive death that awaits him, his desire for knowledge will be reconciled at last with the notion of family that it once annihilated.

Of the two plays, the translation of the *Tyrannos* is the more literal, yet both conform to the plan that Yeats outlined briefly in his preface to the *Tyrannos*: "I put readers and scholars out of my mind and wrote to be sung and spoken. The one thing that I kept in mind was that a word unfitted for living speech, out of its natural order, or unnecessary to our modern technique, would check emotion and tire attention."[10] Indeed, the prose of the two plays, which seems almost too simple if read silently, possesses a fine grace and melody if read aloud. Its literalness comes largely from Jebb's *en face* translation, which the *Times* notice of 1933 informs us Yeats much admired. Yet in the choruses, it is an entirely different matter. Here several considerations seem to have pressed upon the poet. In the first place, he was obviously concerned about their quality as verse, since some were published as parts of books of poetry before the production of the plays. In the second place, he was writing to be sung, not merely read, and this requires a different

[10] W. B. Yeats, *The Variorum Edition of the Plays of W. B. Yeats*, ed. Russell K. Alspach, London, 1966, p. 851.

sense of a line, a greater uniformity of rhythm within the given meter. Yeats sets a modest aim for himself, however: "The main purpose of the chorus," he wrote, "is to preserve the mood while it rests the mind by change of attention" (*Variorum*, p. 851). Yet he did not want to lose the meaning of the words, and the preface puts frequent emphasis upon comprehensibility. Obviously, literalness cannot stand up under such a list of dramatic demands, nor, properly, should it. Yet some editors have declined to use the versions because too many liberties are taken with the Greek. Dudley Fitts comments that "Yeats' sensitive mishandling of the choruses in *King Oedipus* is clearly suspect. . . ."[11] Since the choruses are the crux of what is radically different in Yeats' translations, it is in our interest to examine one of them:

> Endure what life God gives and ask no longer span;
> Cease to remember the delights of youth, travel-
>   wearied aged man;
> Delight becomes death-longing if all longing else be
>   vain.
>
> Even from that delight memory treasures so,
> Death, despair, division of families, all entanglements
>   of mankind grow,
> As that old wandering beggar and these God-hated
>   children know.
>
> In the long echoing streets the laughing dancers throng,
> The bride is carried to the bridegroom's chamber
>   through torchlight and tumultuous song;
> I celebrate the silent kiss that ends short life or long.

[11] Dudley Fitts, ed., *Greek Plays in Modern Translation*, New York, 1947, introduction by Fitts, p. xiv.

Never to have lived is best, ancient writers say;
Never to have drawn the breath of life, never to have
  looked into the eye of day;
The second best's a gay goodnight and quickly turn
  away (*Plays*, p. 353).

This is the sort of chorus from which Schopenhauer built
his theory of tragedy, on the notion that life is a kind
of disease, a disruption that rises up against the fundamental order of nothingness. As we might expect, the
Greek here is fairly spare and forbidding, almost epi-
grammatic in its resignation. Yeats' long lines do little to
convey that atmosphere. In addition, he has translated
only about half the chorus, presumably for the sake of simplicity or economy of musical setting, thereby leaving out
the portions that move from the general to the specific, the
part that sees Oedipus not only as a typical (or archetypal) old man, but also as a particularly afflicted one. This
is the last epode in the version of Robert Fitzgerald:

This is the truth, not for me only,
But for this blind and ruined man.
Think of some shore in the north
Concussive waves make stream
This way and that in gales of winter:
It is like that with him:
The wild wrack breaking over him
From head to foot, and coming on forever;
Now from the plunging down of the sun,
Now from the sunrise quarter,
Now from where the noonday gleams,
Now from the night and the north.[12]

[12] David Grene and Richmond Lattimore, eds., *The Complete
Greek Tragedies: Sophocles* I, New York, n.d., p. 157.

The motion of the total chorus is first, in the strophe, the futility of desire; in the antistrophe, the omnipresence of suffering; and in the epode, pointing to Oedipus, a summarizing metaphor for a man who has suffered everything and yet lives on. By sacrificing the epode, Yeats not only loses a powerful image, but also comes off sounding a little platitudinous, repeating the Greek renunciation of life without counterbalancing it with the dignity of the final metaphor.

In the parts he does translate there is a lingering flavor of Swinburne. In one of the choruses from *King Oedipus*, Yeats almost quotes him: "For death is all the fashion now, till even Death be dead," recalling "For there is no god found stronger than Death, and Death is a sleep" from the "Hymn to Proserpine." In the chorus we are dealing with, this vestigial pre-Raphaelite tone is present most obviously in "I celebrate the silent kiss that ends short life or long," for which there is no equivalent in the Greek. Many of the choruses in Yeats' Sophocles are poetically better than this one, which is admittedly an extreme example. It is hard, however, to find the impact of the original in these lines. Because of the tone and the omissions, they seem to partake more of the Celtic Twilight than of Sophoclean Greek. Since the counterweight of the final metaphor is lacking, there is no sense of compensation, the Greek truth that a man can suffer all this futility and still possess the distinction of a coastline in winter, that he may, in spite of his mortality, become a kind of natural phenomenon.

Without denying the translations their clarity and performability, we can see that Yeats had to embody his tragic impulse in his lyric poetry, not only because this was his primary mode of expression, but also because he could then be choric without the restrictions imposed by the necessity of comprehensibility and musical setting. We have seen that the choric element is weak in *Kohl-haas*, where the major tragic element is the pattern of action. In Melville, we saw Ishmael assume some of the functions of the Greek chorus in his relationship to Ahab as a character and in his relation to the reader as narrator. We have seen how the choric element, no longer orgiastic even in the time of Aeschylus, is now entirely normative, the reactive voice of home and the agrarian values and the stability of the seasons. Or how in Ishmael it can sometimes be the voice of humane common sense. Now, in scrutinizing the lyric poems of Yeats, we will hear the choric voice attempting to remain normative in a world where a tragic conflict of orders is taking place exclusive of characters and heroes. Action will be universalized. The reader—and the poet as well, perhaps—will feel as lonely and isolated as Ahab as he hears this trans-individual tone of prophecy. And he will see tragedy as a force which will mold the ethics and theology of all those who remain to live out the waning of the gyre.

By the time of *The Wild Swans at Coole* (1919), overt references to "the great symbol" of the system appear regularly in the poetry. For example, the volume contains "The Phases of the Moon," which was reprinted in the first edition of *A Vision*. But as the system comes to realization, so too the notion of tragedy grows. A passage from "In Memory of Major Robert Gregory" brings to mind the pivot of Achilles' choice:

Some burn damp faggots, others may consume
The entire combustible world in one small room
As though dried straw, and if we turn about
The bare chimney is gone black out
Because the work had finished in that flare.
Soldier, scholar, horseman, he,
As 'twere all life's epitome.
What made us dream that he could comb grey hair?
                                        (*Poems*, p. 133).

So too the main figure in "An Irish Airman Foresees his Death" feels a twinge of what will be "tragic joy" in his "lonely impulse of delight" at his embraced death:

The years to come seemed waste of breath,
A waste of breath the years behind
In balance with this life, this death   (*Poems*, p. 134).

In "Upon a Dying Lady," he compares his subject with "Achilles, Timor, Babar, Barhaim, all / Who have lived in joy and laughed into the face of Death" (*Poems*, p. 157). *Michael Robartes and the Dancer* (1921), contains the "Prayer for my Daughter," which proclaims that banishment of hatred will restore the soul to "radical innocence" even in the shadow of the gyre's end, and this innocence is not wholly unlike the impulse that allows the dying lady to laugh at death, or that permits Hamlet and Lear the gaiety that Yeats will later find in them.

But I would like to return to a pair of poems, one from *The Tower* (1928), and the other from *The Winding Stair and Other Poems* (1933). These are the two Byzantium poems, first "Sailing to Byzantium," dated 1927, and second, "Byzantium," 1930. Together, the two describe complementary phases of a gyre; they express both poles of the Yeatsian dialectic. To lapse into a technological metaphor, we may say that Yeats' dialectics as expressed in *A Vision* stand to Hegelian dialectics as the rheostatic switch stands to the cradle switch. Though Hegel has only the thesis and its necessary antithesis, Yeats sees in the cosmos a process in which both poles will eventually find total expression. The cycle of Christianity was not always the empty ceremony of the present, for it once produced miracles. So too Greek civilization was not always the considered processional of a Socratic afternoon. In "Sailing to Byzantium" (*Poems*, p. 191), oxymorons like "those dying generations" must be seen not as self-contradictory so much as expressive of process, containing birth, fertility, and the old man watching from the window. The first stanza marks the advent of the new, Dionysian order, filled with "sensual music" and the affirmation of life:

> Fish, flesh, or fowl, commend all summer long
> Whatever is begotten, born, and dies.

In the second stanza, the aged man, being denied a sensual body, tries to affirm by having "soul clap its hands and sing," a curious attribution of bodily parts to the portion of man that is so often considered ethereal and immortal. So it must study "monuments of its own magnificence," which are the same as the "monuments of unaging intellect" of stanza one. The symbol of such an immortality, the city that flourished near the epoch of the full moon, is Byzantium. In the third stanza it is clear that the artisans of these monuments are the artists, or else the artist generalized to a facet of the *spiritus mundi*.

It is this spirit who controls "God's holy fire" which will forge a soul once "fastened to a dying animal" into an eternal artifact. In the fourth stanza we are given that artifact, the gold bird set upon the golden bough to sing to the aristocracy that Yeats identified with the antithetical gyre (*A Vision*, p. 104). This is all very neat, and yet something is wrong. For just as the two components of "dying generations" form a phrase that contains, in the case of either word, its own opposite, so too there are other contradictions in the poem. The soul is described as if it had a body; it is "sick with desire." And to crown it all, in stanza four the *persona* says "Once out of nature I shall never take / My bodily form from any natural thing"—and then he proceeds to take the form of a bird—a forged bird, true, but a bird none the less. It is plain that this poem with its plea for art, the soul, and the immortality of monuments, is planted throughout with the seeds of its opposite. For matters of the soul come to expression through the language of the body, and matter of the body—"dying generations"—are expressed in the language of the narrative *persona*.

"Byzantium" (*Poems*, pp. 243-44) is the returning swing of the pendulum. Here "the unpurged images of day recede"—paradoxically, they recede even though unpurged, even though they will return again in time:

> A starlit or a moonlit dome disdains
> All that man is,
> All mere complexities,
> The fury and the mire of human veins.

Here Yeats is talking about his absolutes, the full moon ("moonlit") which is phase 15 or pure subjectivity, or

the new moon ("starlit") which is phase 1 or pure objectivity. This is the "superhuman" he hails in the second
stanza, and which he calls "death-in-life and life-in-
death," recalling the quotation of Heraclitus which pref-
aces the introduction of the diagram of gyres, "Dying
each other's life, living each other's death" (*A Vision*,
p. 68). The poem thus opens with the opposition of the
uninhabitable extremes of each gyre; it begins in the
total stasis where nothing lives. Then the two points in
the dialectic are seen as mutually dependent for their
meaning. In the third stanza the golden bird from "Sailing
to Byzantium" is transformed into its opposite, the "cocks
of Hades." Thus within the bird which in "Sailing to
Byzantium" was an embodiment of the artifice of the
soul is contained the opposite as well, the horrible cry
of the hell-cocks.

Then, with the advent of the unfed flames on the em-
peror's floor, the standoff of absolutes crumbles, and the
turbulence of the moving gyres resumes. The coming of
the gyre of discord is prophesied in the image of the
dolphins. For although in the first part of the last stanza
we are told that "the smithies break the flood," yet still
at the close the flood continues unabated, with the still
more disturbed image of "That dolphin-torn, that gong-
tormented sea." So that in the course of the two poems
we have seen first an impulse toward artifice, toward
perfect beauty and concord in the aristocratic dominion
of the full moon, followed by a standoff between two
static absolutes, followed again by the resumption of
process and the reassertion of the gyre of the body, discord, and energy (as opposed to still artifact) under the
dominion of the new moon. Here, expressed more elo-

quently than it ever could have been without such elaborate metaphor, is a full panorama of the ethical options open to any member of the human race. Here is the full scope of affirmation and denial that confronted Achilles at the foot of Troy, when he too had to decide on a course, whether he would commit himself to the artifice of eternity, which would make him immortal with all the terrible costs implicit in sacrificing humanity for the existence of a myth; or whether he would return home and surrender to that other mode of living, where life is lived for its own sake, where energy like that of "the dolphin's mire and blood" is celebrated.

We have come, then, to "The Gyres" and "Lapis Lazuli," (*Poems*, pp. 291-93), two from *Last Poems* in which Yeats' notion of tragedy becomes clear and explicit. In "The Gyres," the first two stanzas catalogue the various manifestations of the termination of the gyre. In all cases it is at first a lament for the end of beauty, worth, and graciousness, which turns to joy when the full burden of loss is assumed. "Out of cavern comes a voice, / And all it knows is that one word 'Rejoice!'" In the third stanza, however, another cause for rejoicing in the face of disaster is introduced:

Those that Rocky Face holds dear,
Lovers of horses and of women, shall,
From marble of a broken sepulchre,
Or dark betwixt the polecat and the owl,
Or any rich, dark nothing disinter
The workman, noble and saint, and all things run
On that unfashionable gyre again.

Rocky Face, or the moon, which is the spirit that stands full in the fifteenth phase, will return its figures, the workman, noble, and saint, to their ascendancy again in due time. Though they may seem to perish at the specific moment, driven away in the torrent of blood loosed by the new gyre, their time shall come around again. Now the critic of tragedy must ask whether a cyclic idea of time and history does not destroy the possibility of genuine tragedy, just as it was said for so long that salvation made Christian tragedy impossible. Tragic art depends on the assignment of intrinsic value to earthly life, and intercession from beyond, as in *The Countess Cathleen*, can only compromise it. We do not know what becomes of Ahab after the whale submerges, but we do know that whatever it may be has happened to Ahab, a man ignorant of it as we all are. On the other hand, reincarnation need not be redemptive; it can be, as in certain Eastern religions, merely a repetition of suffering in the world. What keeps Yeats within the tragic scope is that things do not return in particular, but rather in general. The approaching gyre will not be exactly the same as the one that began in 2000 B.C., although its pattern may be the same. The fate of the reincarnated soul in all this is never made certain by the poet. When Yeats writes an elegiac poem, there is never a facile use of doctrines of reincarnation to wash away grief. Similarly, the idea of tragic joy that arises in "The Gyres" is not a mere evasion. Rather, it is a form of that compensation which tends to assert itself in any tragic art. For if there is one thing that must be clear about tragedy, it is that it is never a poetry of loss alone, never a mere dirge for what is

gone. Yeats says only that the things that souls of the
passing gyre loved—their horses, lovers and artifacts—
will not pass from the world altogether. And that they
who loved and lived by them are somehow always part
of them wherever and whenever they recur. This seems
to be a reasonable form of compensation, which neither
takes the sting out of loss nor succumbs entirely to its
power.

"Lapis Lazuli" has five parts, and may be considered
a kind of miniature tragedy in itself. It is the example
par excellence of the tragedy without action in the conventional sense toward which Yeats had been tending for
some years. It was written on the occasion of the presentation to Yeats of an oriental medallion by Harry Clifton,
to whom the poem is dedicated.

> I have heard that hysterical women say
> They are sick of the palette and fiddle-bow,
> Of poets that are always gay,
> For everybody knows or else should know
> That if nothing drastic is done
> Aeroplane and Zeppelin will come out,
> Pitch like King Billy bomb-balls in
> Until the town lie beaten flat.

On the one hand, this opening is an invocation of the visions of blood and war which accompany the approach
of the millennium. On the other hand, it is also a prophecy of a very real war, which by 1939 was already well
under way. Of course, it is also a remembrance of World
War I, with the reference to King Billy meant to recall
Kaiser Wilhelm with his aeroplanes and zeppelins. Yet
the plea for action in the face of such doom is placed in

the mouths of hysterical women, like, perhaps, Maud
Gonne, the unrepenting woman of action, who late in
Yeats' life actually led a picket-line at a performance of
The Playboy of the Western World. As in all tragedies,
there is from the start a presentation of a conflict of orders, here the order of discord and action attacking the
poet's order of concord, construction, and contemplation.

> All perform their tragic play,
> There struts Hamlet, there is Lear,
> That's Ophelia, that Cordelia;
> Yet they, should the last scene be there,
> The great stage curtain about to drop,
> If worthy their prominent part in the play,
> Do not break up their lines to weep.
> They know that Hamlet and Lear are gay;
> Gaiety transfiguring all the dread.
> All men have aimed at, found and lost;
> Black out; Heaven blazing into the head:
> Tragedy wrought to its uttermost.
> Though Hamlet rambles and Lear rages,
> And all the drop-scenes drop at once
> Upon a hundred thousand stages,
> It cannot grow by an inch or an ounce.

Here, suddenly, the point of view shifts from the actual
world to the stage. The pattern of tragedy is summarized
in the tenth and eleventh lines of the stanza: "All men
have aimed at, found and lost; / Black out; Heaven blaz-
ing into the head." This is certainly the essence of the
tragic hero, his rise, fall, and compensation. Yet there is
also a curious, not quite stated gap between the actors
who play the tragic heroes and the heroes themselves.

This is the "they" of the eighth line, who are at once the same as and different from the characters they are playing. The actors are used to universalize the meaning of the passage. It is easier to imagine playing Lear than being Lear. A single person casting himself in a tragic role is capable of "tragedy wrought to the uttermost." Even if it happen to all of us at once, "upon a hundred thousand stages," it is still just as absolute in the individual case as in the coming apocalypse.

> On their own feet they came, or on shipboard,
> Camel-back, horse-back, ass-back, mule-back,
> Old civilisations put to the sword.
> Then they and their wisdom went to rack:
> No handiwork of Callimachus,
> Who handled marble as if it were bronze,
> Made draperies that seemed to rise
> When sea-wind swept the corner, stands;
> His long lamp-chimney shaped like the stem
> Of a slender palm, stood but a day;
> All things fall and are built again,
> And those that build them are gay.

The first two lines of this passage refer to the birth of Christ and the arrival of participants in the adoration. In the system of *A Vision*, the coming of Christ is the event that marks the end of the old gyre, and the beginning of the new gyre of concord. Yet with the terrific changes that accompany the coming of any new gyre, the masterpieces of Callimachus, the pride of the old era, are gone. In the cycle that causes things to fall and be built again, those who rebuild are joyous. But, from the last stanza, we saw that Hamlet and Lear, who are present at the destruction, are also gay. Perhaps there is an implicit identification of falling and building, united as all anti-thetical propositions must necessarily be. But above all it stresses the ultimate optimism of tragedy at all stages, the inherent value both in the carrier of disorder and intruding order, and in the restorer of order. At the same time, the poem does not shy from a full recognition of the destruction and what it has cost the world in glory.

> Two Chinamen, behind them a third,
> Are carved in lapis lazuli,
> Over them flies a long-legged bird,
> A symbol of longevity;
> The third, doubtless a serving-man,
> Carries a musical instrument.

These are the figures who actually appear on the medallion Yeats was given. They are figures of artifact, of course, but unlike the heroes Hamlet and Lear, who have been treated in the first portions of the poem, and who are gay in spite of their participation in "All men have aimed at, found and lost." The Chinamen (china men) are dominated by the long-legged bird who is "a symbol of longevity." These are the figures at the other end of the scale, those who took the opposite path from Achilles' and opted for the long, secure, and anonymous life. The last stanza deals with their relation to tragedy.

> Every discoloration of the stone,
> Every accidental crack or dent,
> Seems a water-course or an avalanche,
> Or lofty slope where it still snows
> Though doubtless plum or cherry-branch
> Sweetens the little halfway house

Those Chinamen climb towards, and I
Delight to imagine them seated there;
There, on the mountain and the sky,
On all the tragic scene they stare.
One asks for mournful melodies;
Accomplished fingers begin to play.
Their eye mid many wrinkles, their eyes,
Their ancient, glittering eyes, are gay.

The apocalypse is recreated in their microcosm by the damage time has done to the stone. These cracks or dents are as great and terrible to them as an avalanche would be in the macrocosm. They stare on the approaching tragedy with detachment, yet of necessity they are involved. They are like a chorus, only suspended in time and space like the figures on Keats' urn; without Dionysian energy, without Apollonian aspiration. Although the music they ask for is to be mournful, it makes them gay. So the delegates of the passive or contemplative life—delegates perhaps of Yeats himself, on the verge not only of the millennium but also of personal death—can participate as well in this tragic joy, and can have their own compensation for the Armageddon at the clash of two orders.

Tragedy without action—can it have any meaning? The question that comes to mind is whether or not Yeats' abstract tragedies of *Last Poems* would have any significance had they not been preceded by *A Vision*, years of dramatic practice, and dialectical poems like the Byzantium pieces. My feeling is that, as Yeats grew older, he attempted to substitute history for action in both his poetic and his dramatic works. Implicitly, a certain mo-

ment of time is selected and frozen, an instant at which
the inevitability of the remaining tragic action is felt as
strongly as if an actual play were acted to a real conclusion. What really happens in a play like *The Resurrection*? If we did not know the history and theology of
the situation, it would be entirely meaningless. So too, if
we do not know Yeats' entire scheme of tragic history,
we are likely to miss the point of the last poems. Tragedy
had become a way of life for him. In the years of Irish
civil conflict, and with the continent torn by World War
I, and in what he foresaw of the coming of World War II,
there was a pattern of doom which he felt could make
every man a tragic hero, or at any rate a kind of chorus
member. And yet it is to his credit that he did not attempt to establish tragedy as an abstract philosophy, re-
moving it from literature and annihilating its meaning
with the formlessness of quotidian experience and random disaster. In order to convey the sense of tragedy he
had arrived at, he had to construct a system which, almost in a Mallarméan way, would turn history first into
literature. *A Vision* gives poetic form to all the experience of all mankind, or so it was intended to do. Once
that form had been given, and the antinomies of the matter were established, then it was possible to treat history
poetically in new and striking ways; at the same time it
was possible to write a tragedy whose action is the
time we are living in, whose characters are all of us.

5 Classical Analogy: Giraudoux versus Faulkner

///

There are two basic strategies for twentieth-century writers approaching the problem of tragedy. We might call them "imitation" and "incarnation"—tragedy by reference to one previous, usually classical work, as against the creation of an entirely modern tragedy which owes its tragic qualities to no single source. In general, the imitative sort tends to be written for the stage—the plays of Cocteau, Giraudoux, Anouilh, Sartre, as well as certain of Eliot's and O'Neill's—whereas the second type is found in any number of genres, in the novel in *All the King's Men*, on the stage in *Long Day's Journey into Night*, in the cinema in *Citizen Kane*.

Frank Kermode, in *The Sense of an Ending*, makes an instructive distinction between myth and fiction. Fiction for Kermode is a tentative explanation of something, an account punctuated by "as if" to which we give conditional, temporary assent. The truth or falsity of the fiction is beside the point. "The only relevant question," Kermode quotes Nietzsche as saying, is "how far the opinion is life-furthering, life-preserving, species-preserving."[1] Myth, on the other hand, is fiction grown old, become codified and tyrannical. Kermode writes, "Myths are the agents of stability, fictions are agents of change.

---

[1] Kermode, Frank, *The Sense of an Ending*, London, 1968, p. 37.

Myth calls for absolute, fictions for conditional assent"
(p. 39).

The writer who uses just one myth or literary precedent to organize a work runs a signal risk. If he uses
Apollo, Christ or Caesar, he incurs a burden of tradition
that may tend to hamper his flexibility. He risks having
the whole of his fiction poured into the mold of the myth,
seen only within its confines. When in *The Old Man and
the Sea* Hemingway drew a parallel between Santiago
and Jesus, the result was a destruction of his fiction by
the necessity of reading it as a restatement. The analogy
made his story brittle. When Eliot ended *The Family
Reunion* with the line "May they rest in peace," it was
no longer Eliot writing, but rather an older hand per-
mitting little deviation.

One measure that authors take to protect themselves
from the tyranny of myth is a technique that might be
called partial analogy, in which a character shares only
some characteristics or circumstances with a mythical
figure. In *The Family Reunion*, Harry is found in a
situation analogous to that of Orestes, so that by extension Mary fills the place of Electra and Amy that of
Clytemnestra. Yet Harry, though he sees his Furies, does
not conspire with Mary to murder Amy. Rather, the
murder is dislocated from the myth so that, during his
wanderings, Harry has already killed his wife. Deviation
from the myth creates a healthy tension, as of disobedi-
ence. It is possible then to take the modern character
somewhat on his own terms.

Yet this much deviation itself fails to restore freedom
to the fiction. The reader may have the feeling that the

device is contrived by the author in reaction to the myth; that, with all the cunning of a child, the character knew what he ought to do, and then deliberately did something else. Then the myth, like the household rule the child violates, may enforce itself all the more strictly thereafter. The problem is that the character who is given the analogue both is and is not the character in the myth. In so far as he is, any illusion of free will is impaired. There is a control upon him from outside, from some place beyond the bounds of the fiction. How can a writer get the resonance of an analogue without paying the price of his fiction's autonomy and fluidity?

For an example of the first type of tragedy, the imitative sort, let us consider the *Electre* of Jean Giraudoux (1937). In this work, the initial step taken by the author to avoid rigidity is the selection of a double source. Some of his material comes from Aeschylus' *Libation Bearers*, some from Euripides' *Elektra*. We have, for example, a trio of Furies who are intended to refer to the *Oresteia*, yet from Euripides we have the plot to marry Elektra to a farmer. In addition, new characters are introduced side by side with the traditional ones: we have not only Electre, Oreste, Egisthe, Clytemnestre, but also a local judge and his wife, who are intended as satires on the French bourgeoisie, and an omniscient beggar. The Eumenides are seen as girls who grow from childhood to maturity in the course of the play. There is also no real chorus, since the Furies speak in tandem. Instead, the beggar provides a running commentary which, in time, becomes narration.

Of course, these structural changes are not sufficient

to free the drama from its source, so further changes have to be instituted. The most striking of these is in diction. Instead of the complex and elevated speech of Greek tragedy, we have Eumenides who go through elaborate rituals of childlike sarcasm, the narrating beggar appearing drunk and babbling about hedgehogs, and Egisthe walking into a continuing quarrel between the judge and his wife, an exchange that borrows its style of repartee from domestic comedy. Likewise, the plot is altered to provide new details about the murder of Agamemnon—Clytemnestre soaps the stairs so he will slip—and to include an entanglement of the domestic quarrels with the fate of the major characters, and, most drastic of all, to have Egisthe and Clytemnestre killed by Oreste in conspiracy with a mob of rebellious beggars, and at the close to have the city overrun by an army of invading Corinthians.

A good deal of this "updating" is done for political reasons. The internal strife in Argos, which is France, has thrown both domestic and state functions into disarray. The state cannot rule, the family has no authority, beggars (Communists) revolt in the streets, and under the banner of Freud, children rise up against their parents. Electre has an overt Electra complex, and there is more than a hint of incest between brother and sister. In every case of a family tie, except for that of Oreste and Electre, there is nothing but argument. Speech is so permeated with legalisms that it is impossible to get at the source of problems, or see any solutions. The playwright's point is obviously that if France does not deal with her internal crises, she will be defenseless against the invasion of the Corinthians (Germans), after which no one—neither the Electres nor the Clytemnestres—will be any better off.

Admirable as such an alert seems, particularly in retrospect, it is not sufficiently explicit nor endemic to the structure of the play to allow for flexibility of character. Instead, Giraudoux's device is this: since the characters must be reduced in stature anyway, walking as they are in the footsteps of their Greek sources, the playwright will anticipate this reduction by voluntarily reducing from the start, by making the language and behavior of the characters so unbecoming to their "originals" that the expectations of the audience are unsettled. Then, against these self-determined odds, perhaps they will grow into their analogues on their own terms, perhaps this petty creature who stands in the place of Electra will slowly acquire her proper status if she makes only a limited claim to it in the first place. Accordingly, an idea of "se déclarer" or "self-declaration" is developed.[2] This concept, which calls to mind the Existentialist doctrine that "existence precedes essence," is used as an artificial aid to help the characters gain stature. Egisthe, for example, reappearing in the second act, has undergone a moment of self-declaration and become truly a king. He is "infiniment plus majestueux et serein qu'au premier acte. Très haut, un oiseau plane au-dessus de lui" (p. 163). ("Infinitely more majestic and serene than in the first act. High overhead, a bird hovers above him.") This may be a faint echo of those scenes in the Odyssey where Athena gives Odysseus additional height and grandeur at points

[2] Giraudoux, Jean, *Electre*, Paris, 1937, p. 51 and all references to this edition.

of crisis, except that in this case the cause is not divine. Rather, it is on the one hand a function of the individual in his situation, and on the other hand an all-too-apparent function of authorial intrusion. In terms of the plot, these moments occur when, in Hegelian fashion, characters become identified with something greater than themselves. For example, Egisthe "declares himself" when he becomes one with the existing order, the consolidation of the mediocre and fallible against internal disruption and outside invasion. And Electre "declares herself" at the moment when she realizes her identity with "la justice intégrale," or "total justice" (p. 32).

The artificiality of such a device is really determined by the strength or weakness of the choric element in the play. With a clear body of collective feeling—not to mention collective utterance or tribal commitment—these leaps to essence or self-realization would have a convincing ground of origin, and there would be a clear body of energy which the characters might tap to be so empowered. But in fact there is none. The Eumenides never develop into anything more than sarcastic children, even given their ability to foresee. Foresight must not be confused with prophecy, any more than multiplicity with collectivity. Throughout the play, they are only gadflies who annoy people with the truth of their actions, always in a precious and nastily offhand way. Similarly, the beggar, whose omniscience and philosophical bent might allow him some choric properties, becomes in time a mere narrator whose foreknowledge gives the action an even more stultified predetermination. At one point he goes so far as to narrate an event—the murder of Egisthe— before it has actually taken place (p. 216). One might

attempt to excuse Giraudoux on the grounds that there is
no choric tradition in France, that their classical tragedy
was more classical than tragic. Yet this does not explain
away the two fundamental deficiencies of the play: first,
that in a drama designed to alert the French to the coming
of national disaster there is no sense of the collective or
the national; second, that the lack of endemic energy in
the play allows the rigidity of the myth to take hold,
making the alterations in plot seem trivial and the characters wooden or debased.

Indeed, it is possible to generalize this criticism to all
the "imitative" modern tragedies. Without a chorus or
any equivalent, *Mourning Becomes Electra* is stiff, defeated and long-winded. Even in the plays of Sartre, designed to recast the old myths in Existentialist format,
characters like Oreste in *Les Mouches* take on the guilt
of others only as individual acts. The presence of a crowd
on stage once again fails to create a feeling of true collectivity, although the Furies are less preciously conceived than in Giraudoux. By and large, the imitative
premise in modern tragedy has proven to be an unsound
gambit. Rarely has the stature of a character grown by
his identity with a myth as much as he has suffered by it;
and never has an action developed an integrity when
brought into conflict with a classical counterpart. Perhaps this is only a result of the narrowness with which
many writers have approached the problem, trying to
make a social, philosophical, or political point at the ex-
pense of the complexity of the source. Or perhaps the
cultural meshing of the twentieth century with classical
Greece is in fact a matter too delicate to be solved by
noting the relaxation of Christian orthodoxy, and assum-

ing some sort of continuity of which the Christian era was only a prolonged interruption.

In any event, the possibilities inherent in non-allusive or eclectically allusive modern tragedy seem much greater. In the case of *Absalom, Absalom!*, Faulkner, without shying away from analogy, is successful in avoiding the rigid hand of myth upon his fiction. W. M. Frohock, for one, criticizes the book for its "quality of improvisation."[3] Yet this quality is a real achievement considering the richness of analogy on the surface of the novel. In the first place, following the lead of the title, Sutpen is King David, who attempted to found a dynasty but whose sons were destroyed. Yet Sutpen's band of followers resembles that attributed to Absalom himself in 2 Sam. 14: 11: "And with Absalom went two hundred men out of Jerusalem, that were called; and they went in their simplicity, and they knew not any thing." Sutpen is also Adam, who has come down from a classless land in the mountains, where there is no property and where all virtue is demonstrable in physical terms, into a land where his poverty excludes him from a plantation-house door. He is Agamemnon, gone to war while a woman named Clytemnestra awaits him. He is Odysseus, whose Penelope is a mare.[4] He is Jason, sowing his "fecundity of dragons' teeth" (p. 62). He is Abraham (p. 285), and a Faustus grown old. It is implied that he has sold his soul (p. 180). By extension, analogues may be assigned to other characters according to their positions in family

[3] Frohock, W. M., *The Novel of Violence in America*, Boston, 1957, p. 144.

[4] Faulkner, William, *Absalom, Absalom!*, New York, 1962, p. 285. All references to this edition.

structure, for example Bon as Amnon, Henry as Orestes or Absalom or Telemachus, Judith as Electra, and so forth. In addition, characters are sometimes given independent antecedents: Bon as Lancelot (p. 320), Rosa Coldfield as Eve (p. 144), or Cassandra (p. 177), and so on.

Rather than compounding the dangers and difficulties of analogizing, this multiplicity creates other problems. If too much of it protrudes onto the surface, the result can be meaninglessness and obscurity, as in some of Pound's less successful *Cantos*. Or else the resonating quality which is the reason for the analogies may be alternated and lost. On the other hand, the influence of numerous myths creates a situation like that of a country with many governments: so many contrary imperatives are given that people ignore them and in general do what they please. Faulkner's fiction is left free to develop on its own terms, and the characters are permitted their Jamesian right to behave. Sutpen does not think of himself as Agamemnon. If he fails to build a dynasty, he fails not because King David or Agamemnon failed, but because of the intrinsic forces that rise out of the fiction itself. Likewise in *Moby-Dick*, the numerous implied analogies given to Ahab do not hamper the development of the book. The fact that he is at once Prometheus, Faust, and Lear leaves him freer to be himself than if he were any one of those mythic figures alone. He is still free to exclaim, as he does, that "Ahab is forever Ahab."

It is best, then, to consider what is tragic in *Absalom, Absalom!* apart from the fact that it makes reference to the *Oresteia*. If there is any affinity, it will have to be found on a deeper level than that of the action, since action, *per se*, is something Faulkner deliberately makes secondary in his work. Following an Emersonian view of history, in which the reactions of those who study it are more important than the actual facts, Faulkner prints as an appendix to the book a bone-dry factual summary of the events that take place, along with terse synopses of the characters' lives. Since some of the scenes are rendered more than once by the narrators, with each including different details according to his personal temperament, and since the chronology of the text is so disrupted, it is clearly out of the spirit of the book to make a Hegelian analysis of the plot. Certain facets of the action are, however, interesting, since they follow many of the general patterns that, as we have observed earlier, are standard for tragedy.

Into a state of order and tranquility comes a figure who presents a rival and disruptive order. In a town like Jefferson, full of small businessmen and farmers, a man appears who would declare himself a king. Yet he does not move directly into the heart of town, nor try deliberately to shatter the local order; rather, he buys his property at the edge of town, and stages a rebellion like Satan's in *Paradise Lost* or the South's in the Civil War. It is not an attack on what is; it is an attempt to create an alternative order that will outshine the previous one. Sutpen's desire, as he expresses it, is to set right the inadequacies of a society that would force him to enter a plantation-house by the slave-entry simply on account of his poverty. He reacts against this injustice, not by egalitarianism, but by a species of personal aristocracy. Therefore there is no direct clash between the orders, only a tense suspicion. In Hegelian terms, the lack of identifiable absoluteness on either part might lead to a rejection of the book as tragedy because of insufficient inevitability and universality. Applying Nietzsche's *Die Geburt der Tragödie*, however, leads to strikingly different conclusions.

For Nietzsche the structural and dynamic center of tragedy is the chorus. As primary embodiments of the Dionysian spirit, it is out of their song that the stage-characters are said to rise like mere dreams. Nietzsche saw the chorus as the eternal reality, the characters as transient and individual illusions created as a kind of by-product of their collective energy. To apply Nietzsche to a prospectively tragic work, we must first locate a chorus, or a source of choric energy that will somehow be its equivalent. There are three possible equivalents in *Absalom, Absalom!*, not by any means mutually exclusive, and these are first, the townspeople; second, Sutpen's slaves; and third, the narrators themselves.

In the first case, that of the people of Jefferson, Faulkner deliberately suggests their choric function in the following passage: "The stranger's name went back and forth among the places of business and of idleness and among the residences in steady strophe and antistrophe: *Sutpen. Sutpen. Sutpen. Sutpen*" (p. 32). The idea of a chorus of townspeople is frequent in classical tragedy, and in *Absalom!*, with its specific Aeschylean references it brings the *Agamemnon* to mind immediately. There, however, the chorus sings a paean of glory to the returning hero, here they only murmur with hostility. But one choric function they do fulfill is that of naming. The act of naming on the part of a chorus individuates the person named, singles him out from the collectivity, and thus gives him the first requisite of heroism. The transience of names recalls Nietzsche's idea of the illusory quality of the Apollonian. Quentin's childhood, we are told, was full of such names: "His very body was an empty hall echoing with sonorous defeated names; . . . He was a barracks filled with stubborn back-looking ghosts . . ." (p. 12). Before Sutpen comes, his name is not certain. "He came here with a horse and two pistols and a name which nobody ever heard before, knew for certain was his own any more than the horse was his own or even the pistols . . ." (p. 15). The townspeople carry out this task of naming, and thus they are part of the choric component of the work.

The second possibility, Sutpen's black slaves, is quite different, since these Haitians do not speak the same language as the Jeffersonians. They are like an Anglo-Saxon *comitatus*, or Lear's band of retainers. They are referred to in language not wholly unlike that which Nietzsche uses in talking of the Greek chorus: "Anyone could look at those negroes of his and tell that they may have come (and probably did) from a much older country than Virginia or Carolina but it wasn't a quiet one" (p. 17). The suggestion of antiquity brings to mind the Dionysian antecedents of tragic choruses, the ritual bands that are recalled (however fictitiously) in sources like the *Bacchae*. Full of a terrible vitality that somehow antedates the Olympians, these cults, in spite of the ethical meaning that they seem to have acquired by the time of Aeschylus, still conjure up images of punishment by dismemberment and frank, earthy sexuality. Because of their alien tongue, Sutpen's slaves seem to express themselves in primarily physical ways. And Sutpen, the hero, as if in order to draw off some of that primal power, wrestles with them in their own style from time to time, as if he were performing a ritual obeisance to his source of strength.

But the third possible equivalent of a chorus, the narrators themselves, seems the most compelling of them all. Ilse DuSoir Lind, in "The Design and Meaning of *Absalom, Absalom!*", points out that "all the narrators speak in two voices—their own idiom, when engaged in casual conversation with each other, and the highly stylized orations in which they serve as narrators of the legend."[5] Greek choruses also have two voices. One is the "highly stylized" voice of the odes, the other the more colloquial, elliptical voice used in the dialogue with stage figures, which is called *stichomythia*. Faulkner's characters lose their individual tone to a large extent, so that if we open to a random page of the novel it is difficult to tell who is talking. Like members of Greek choruses, they talk about themselves much less frequently than they talk about the heroic figures, speculating on what they have done, and reacting to them. Like choruses, they are timeless. As in the *Agamemnon*, they survey the history of the family in question, and make it cohere, perceiving it as a simultaneity. At one point, Mr. Compson takes the first person plural: ". . . we see dimly people, the people in whose living blood and seed we ourselves lay dormant and waiting, in this shadowy attenuation of time possessing now heroic proportions, performing their acts

[5] Lind, Ilse DuSoir, "The Design and Meaning of *Absalom, Absalom!*", *PMLA*, LXX (Dec. 1955), p. 290.

of simple passion and simple violence, impervious to time and inexplicable" (p. 101).

Regarding the narrators as the chorus is also helpful for understanding the apparent artificiality of the language. Frohock points out that we must abandon conventional notions of realism to recognize it for what it is—the essential poetry of a universal human response. Walter Slatoff, in "The Edge of Order,"[6] makes an almost Hegelian defense of Faulkner's oxymorons, syntactic upsets and *non sequiturs*. The language, Slatoff says, must be ambiguous, if possible as rich in vagueness as poetry, in order that the intellect may cease to wrestle with the contradictions and may cede the power of synthesis to the emotions. Something quite similar might be said for Aeschylus. In his choric passages, the Greek word order and syntax are often strained to the breaking point. Seen in this vatic tradition of choric writing, the language used by Faulkner in *Absalom, Absalom!* seems absolutely just.

To replace a conventional form of narration with a chorus is certain to alter the nature of the hero. Indeed, it is difficult to say that the reader comes to know Sutpen well. The only words of his that we hear are filtered down through layers of hearsay, and at times he seems almost as vague as he is large. Quentin, for example, quotes these supposed words of Sutpen which come to him in paraphrase through his grandfather and father: "Destiny had fitted itself to him, to his innocence, his pristine apti-

---

[6] Slatoff, Walter, "The Edge of Order: The Pattern of Faulkner's Rhetoric," in *William Faulkner: Three Decades of Criticism*, ed. Frederick J. Hoffman and Olga Vickery, New York, 1960.

tude for platform drama and childlike heroic simplicity"
(p. 246). He is a hero of an older time, one of the heroes,
as Mr. Compson says, "of that day and time, of a dead
time; people too as we are, and victims too as we are, but
victims of a different circumstance, simpler and therefore, integer for integer, larger, more heroic and the
figures therefore more heroic too, not dwarfed and involved but distinct, uncomplex who had the gift of lov-
ing once or dying once instead of being diffused . . ."
(p. 89). This is the book's expression of Achilles' choice,
abstracted though it may be from Sutpen's actual decision on the matter. Sutpen's decision to live apart from
the normative world of the town, in his self-built mansion of baronial splendor, Faulkner tells us, allies him to
the heroes of a prior time, allies him, perhaps, to the heroes of the Greek stage. Rosa has the sensation of never
having seen Sutpen's true face, and in the explanation of
this phenomenon the parallel becomes explicit: "Miss
Rosa had not seen him a hundred times in her whole life.
And what she saw then was just that ogre-face of her
childhood seen once and then repeated at intervals and
on occasions which she could neither count nor recall,
like the mask in Greek tragedy, interchangeable not only
from scene to scene, but from actor to actor . . ." (p. 62).

The manner in which Sutpen achieves heroic stature
through the voice of the chorus is almost a paradigm of
what Nietzsche said is supposed to happen: ". . . sind wir
jetzt zu der Einsicht gekommen, dass die Scene immer ein
Räthsel blieb, sammt der Action im Grunde und ur-
sprünglich nur als *Vision* gedacht wurde, dass die 'Reali-
tät' eben der Chor ist, der die Vision aus sich erzeugt
und von ihr mit der ganzen Symbolik des Tanzes, des

Tones und des Wortes redet."[7] ("But now we realize
that the scene, complete with the action, was basically
thought of merely as a *vision*; the chorus is the only
'reality' and generates the vision, speaking of it with
the entire symbolism of dance, tone and words.")[8] This
vision "ist der apollinische Traumeszustand, in dem die
Welt des Tages sich verschleiert und eine neue Welt,
deutlicher, verständlicher, ergreifender als jene und doch
schattengleicher, in fortwährendem Wechsel sich un-
serem Auge neu gebiert. Demgemäss erkennen wir in
der Tragödie einen durchgreifenden Stilgegensatz: Spra-
che, Farbe, Beweglichkeit, Dynamik der Rede treten
in der dionysischen Lyrik des Chors und anderseits in
der apollinische Traumwelt der Scene als völlig ge-
sonderte Sphären des Ausdrucks aus einander."[9] (This
vision "is the Apollonian state of dreams in which the
world of the day becomes veiled, and a new world,
clearer, more understandable, more moving than the
everyday world and yet more shadowy, presents itself to
our eyes in continual rebirths. Accordingly, we recognize in tragedy a sweeping opposition of styles: the language, color, mobility and dynamics of speech fall apart
into the Dionysian lyrics of the chorus and, on the other
hand, the Apollonian dreamworld, and become two utterly different spheres of expression.")[10] In these terms,
Absalom, Absalom! is as exemplary a tragedy as any

[7] Nietzsche, Friedrich, *Gesammelte Werke*, 3er band, München, 1920, p. 62.
[8] Nietzsche, Friedrich, *The Birth of Tragedy and The Case
of Wagner*, trans. Walter Kaufmann, New York, 1967, p. 65.
[9] Nietzsche, *Gesammelte Werke*, 3er band, p. 64.
[10] Nietzsche, *The Birth of Tragedy and The Case of Wagner*,
p. 66.

Nietzsche ever knew. The figure of Sutpen first appears rising out of the voice of Rosa Coldfield: ". . . and the voice not ceasing but vanishing into and then out of long intervals like a stream, a trickle running from patch to patch of dried sand, and the ghost mused with shadowy docility as if it were the voice that he haunted where a more fortunate one would have had a house. Out of quiet thunderclap he would abrupt (man-horse-demon) upon a scene peaceful and decorous as a schoolprize watercolor, faint sulphur reek still in hair clothes and beard, with grouped behind him his band of wild niggers like beasts half-tamed to walk upright among men, in attitudes wild and reposed" (p. 8). The ghosts that come from the voices of the chorus are, almost as Nietzsche described them, "clearer, more comprehensible," like the simpler heroes of the "dead Time" that Mr. Compson praises. Nietzsche tells us too that in the Apollonian state "the daylight world is veiled." So too "Mr. Compson said, 'Maybe even the light of day, let alone this—' he indicated the single globe stained and bugfouled from the long summer . . . 'would be too much for it, for them' " (p. 89).

In Nietzschean fashion, then, *Absalom, Absalom!* represents a return to the fundamental state of tragedy, the era prior to Aeschylus when the chorus was quite literally the source. Out of the early choric odes, perhaps a single member of the choric body would step forward to recount a myth or a piece of history. Aristotle tells us that Thespis was the first to introduce an actor, by which we assume he means a player wholly discrete from the chorus. In those early days, the odes and perhaps the narration of the leader *were* the action. The tale that was told, the epic selection or historical incident, was clearly secondary. So too in Faulkner's novel Sutpen emerges from and is reabsorbed into the collective song. Instead of worrying the problem of tragedy into the one-to-one confrontation of imitative tragedy, Faulkner finds his hero in the chorus. Where Sutpen is ultimately an artifact— "a face whose flesh had the appearance of pottery" (p. 33)—the members of the chorus are consummately human. Quentin and Shreve, particularly, struggle to balance their individualities against the great collective magnetism. They sit up late at night in a cold dormitory at Harvard, with Quentin recounting the tale to his Canadian roommate almost against his own will, and then, in time, Shreve, who knows none of the participants first hand, begins to narrate himself, joining, merging with the song, becoming part of the chorus.

So Shreve and Quentin become merged, closer, become brothers like the brothers in the tale they are narrating. "That was why it did not matter to either of them which one did the talking . . ." (p. 316). Then the two, having become brothers in the chorus, become merged with the figures they themselves are creating: "So that now it was not two but four of them riding the two horses through the dark over the frozen December ruts of that Christmas Eve: four of them and then just two— Charles-Shreve and Quentin-Henry . . ." (p. 334). And in the perishing of the mythic men and women in their story, they draw strength, they draw the necessary compensation for their loss of self, for their cold nights of telling. Their collectivity becomes, as it so often does in tragedy, generalized to the collectivity of the tribe. It begins with Shreve's catechism on the role of the past in the South. "What is it? something you live and breathe in like air? a kind of vacuum filled with wraithlike and indomitable anger and pride and glory at and in happenings that occurred and ceased fifty years ago?" [. . .] "You cant understand it. You would have to be born there," answers Quentin (p. 361). But Shreve in his own way does understand; understands that in a choric song the singers extend their consciousness upward as if onto a stage, creating a sudden individuation, a Sutpen who appears to take on individual life for a time before, transient as the words that created him, he lapses back again into the collectivity of the people of Jefferson, into the "air" of the South.

The book ends with Quentin's affirmation, after so much doubt and pain, of the race, the tribe, the South. With his words ("I dont hate it! I dont hate it!") the reader cannot help but feel that he has experienced something momentous, something greater than the differentiated heroism of Sutpen would justify. Perhaps this is the evasive *catharsis*, feeling for the multitude, the species-preservation that succeeds the fall of the hero who tried to transcend it, tried to be more human. Thinking of the South, we might simply repeat the words that Nietzsche applied to the Greeks: "Wie viel musste dies Volk leiden, um so schön werden zu können!"[11]—how much they must have suffered, to become so beautiful.

[11] Nietzsche, *Gesammelte Werke*, 3er band, p. 165.

6 Choric Equivalents in Modern Drama

///

The dilemma is stated by T. S. Eliot in "Poetry and Drama":

> [The Furies] must, in future, be omitted from the cast, and be understood to be visible only to certain of my characters, and not to the audience. We tried every possible manner of presenting them. We put them on the stage, and they looked like uninvited guests who had strayed in from a fancy dress ball. We concealed them behind a gauze, and they suggested a still out of a Walt Disney film. We made them dimmer, and they looked like shrubbery just outside the window. I have seen other expedients tried: I have seen them signaling from across the garden, or swarming onto the stage like a football team, and they are never right. They never succeeded in being either Greek goddesses or modern spooks. But their failure is merely a symptom of the failure to adjust the ancient with the modern.[1]

The anecdotes that are told about the initial performance of *The Eumenides* and the horror that the sight of the Furies inspired seem inconceivable to us today. What do we have in our culture that is so terrifying? Our terrors lack focus, they are so massive and eschatological as to defy personification. But it is not only terror that is far from us in its embodied form. It would be equally diffi-

[1] T. S. Eliot, *On Poetry and Poets*, New York, 1961, p. 90.

cult to present a convincing chorus of any kind, whether
to express fear, joy, wisdom, or civic feeling. Individualism is too highly developed in us as a people, and has
been so for centuries. As early as Elizabethan times, there
could be no directly represented chorus. Shakespeare was
an astute enough practical dramatist to find other ways
of dealing with the need, a need common to all tragedy,
for a full expression of the collective impulse. In the
comic scenes he accomplished the widening of social per-
spective that the Greeks achieved, with choruses drawn
from respected but ordinary walks of city life. For the
widening of metaphysical significance in the Greek
choric odes, he substituted the soliloquy, and had an individual figure expand in spirit to express universal sentiments, timeless truths and poetic distance. There were
also occasional crowd scenes to simulate the density of
the urban population. The elegance of the Attic stage
was now too obvious. Two or three strategies had to be
employed where the Greeks needed but one.

Dramatic writing in our own century has had to shoul-
der the additional burden of an increased consciousness
of the importance of the chorus, which at earlier periods
of critical history had been regarded as ornamental. The
main source for this renewed seriousness is of course
Nietzsche, who put forth the notion not only of the integrity of the chorus's role within the structure of the
play, but even of its primacy. What might have been dismissed as a deviant opinion was not to be ignored after
the scholarly writings of Jane Harrison and Gilbert Murray, who sought archaeological and anthropological evidence for the proposition of *Die Geburt der Tragödie*.
A certain self-consciousness arose among dramatists. If

they accepted Nietzsche's tenets, how were they to seek and recapture this primal impulse that would give their drama a stature great enough to compete with the ancient in immediacy?

There have been as many solutions to that problem as there have been playwrights. We have seen that it is not impossible for a modern writer to recreate tragic *action*. We have also seen the curious success of a novel, where a play failed by direct attack. A complete survey of the question would require more space than can be given here, yet a few examples will probably serve to provide a general picture of the various options that have been tried in the past few decades.

The choruses in *Murder in the Cathedral* are constructed directly on classical models. They are satisfying as poetry to be read, and demonstrate a developed awareness of the problems and traditions of Greek choric writing. The first chorus has the women of Canterbury awaiting the return of the archbishop. The undoubtedly conscious model here is the opening chorus of the *Agamemnon*. Eliot's women of Canterbury lament the "seven years since the archbishop left us"[2] just as the Argive elders remember the ten years since the departure of Agamemnon. The atmosphere of prolonged waiting that Aeschylus conveys from the opening lines of the play is well imitated. Where the Greek chorus combines a mythopoeic function with an elementality of imagery, Eliot must settle for a rather easier identification of the chorus with concerns of an agrarian kind. This is very much in keeping with the conclusions of the neo-Nietz-

[2] T. S. Eliot, *Complete Poems and Plays*, New York, n.d., p. 176.

scheans. The names of the months are invested with a mystical weight, the development of the seasons and of vegetation replaces events as such:

> For us, the poor, there is no action,
> But only to wait and to witness (p. 177).

The chorus thus represents an anonymous and stable order of the soil, of home. The action of the play intrudes upon this: "Now I fear disturbance of the quiet seasons" (p. 176). The second chorus simplifies this complex of associations into a plea for an unobtrusive and mediocre way of life against which the events of the tragedy will be aptly cataclysmic: "We do not wish anything to happen" (p. 180).

Eliot's strategy is simple enough. Portraying "the small folk drawn into the pattern of fate" (p. 181), he wants to give as clear an embodiment as possible to the polarities of Achilles' choice. By as direct an imitation of the Greeks as the modern stage will allow, he places a primacy on the choric mode that both begins and concludes his play. The attempt to align the traditional concerns of the chorus with his own interest in Christianity is of course dubious, but it must be admitted that it is a sophisticated attempt. Especially in the closing chorus, this alignment dwells upon the similarities of Christ and Dionysos, their death and resurrection, their association with the poor, their closeness to the earth. In fact, this element of *Murder in the Cathedral* might be entirely successful were it not for the rather leisurely rhythms of the verse, and its tone of resignation and quietude, which would obviously be difficult to maintain in unison. It would of course be possible to perform the play with members of the chorus speaking one at a time, and reciting together only for repeated or closing passages.

The fact remains, though, that there is no tradition of choric appearance for the modern theatre. Eliot's critical statements reinforce his practical elimination of the chorus. In *The Family Reunion*, a chorus made up of four characters from the drama replaces an independent group, and they, not the mute Furies, constitute the generalizing, collectivizing element of the play. In *The Cocktail Party*, there is no equivalent at all. Eliot should at any rate be given credit for trying what most other dramatists have skirted.

Two years before *Murder in the Cathedral*, Federico Garcia Lorca sought a choric equivalent in his use of archetypes in *Bodas de Sangre* (1933). To begin with, he compromised the individuality of the stage characters by naming only one of them, Leonardo, who is the bearer of disorder. The rest are known only by their social identities, La Madre, La Novia, La Suegra, and so forth. They flicker back and forth between existence as actors and re-actors. The knife, modern analogue of the traditional Apollonian sword, becomes an emblem for participation in events, and the emblem for the sum of those events—the action—is the horse.

> Oye. No hay más que un caballo en el mundo,
>   y es éste (p. 1160).[3]

> (Listen. There is only one horse in the world,
>   and this is it.)

[3] Federico Garcia Lorca, *Obras Completas*, Madrid, 1954.

The archetypal nature of the characters, coupled with the fundamental quality of these emblems, gives the play a sense of ritual enaction rather than action. The outcome is visible far in advance, not only because of parallel instances in the past of the people, recounted as they are by various older characters, but also because of the tradition of family feud dramas, miniature cases of civil war, which characterizes tragedy from the *Oresteia* on. The sense of repetition recreates the cyclic conception of time endemic to Greek choruses as to all agrarian people. Everything that happens has happened before. This serves as equivalent of the mythic history recounted by Attic choruses as background to the events at hand.

All this takes place in the dialogue itself. The resonance that choric song lends to incident is built by Lorca into the very conversation that constitutes the bulk of the play's time. But there is more. Inserted into the text, in places where a full-scale choric ode would seem to be indicated, are lyrics spoken either by characters or by even more archetypal figures like the personified Luna or the beggar-woman who stands for death itself. The lyric, which exists out of time, has the same effect as a choric ode in bringing the forward motion of events to a reflective halt. Even the lullabies and songs in praise of the bride are dark with foreboding. The speakers of these lyrics, even when they are only servants, transcend their individual identities and become one with the larger machinations of the ritual:

> *Criada*: (En voz alta.)
> ¡Prepara el vino!
>
>   (En voz poética)

Galana.
Galana de la tierra,
mira cómo el agua pasa.
Porque llega tu boda
recógete las faldas
y bajo el ala del novio
nunca salgas de tu casa.
Porque el novio es un palomo
con todo el pecho de brasa
y espera el campo el rumor
de la sangre derramada.
Giraba,
giraba la rueda
y el agua pasaba (p. 1134).

(Servant-woman: [In a loud voice.]
  Prepare the wine!

      [In a poetic voice]

Elegant.
Most elegant in the world,
see how the water is passing.
Because your wedding arrives
gather in the skirts
and under the groom's wing
never leave your house.
For the groom is a dove
with all his breast of live coals
and the field hopes for a rumor
of spilt blood.
Was turning,
the wheel was turning
and the water was passing.)

Here the servant-woman fades in and out of the choric mode, turning abruptly back and forth from the preparations for the wedding to her meditation on the nature of all marriage. Two things are in motion. First, the water, which is the passage of chronological time, the time of the action, the time that will bring the event, the wedding, to pass. Then there is the wheel, or cyclic time, the time that brings weddings around again and again, the time within which ritual works. Although the groom is called a dove, this is immediately countered with the assertion that he will spill blood. Naturally, there is a dual sense to that as well, the same dual sense that the title of the piece possesses, that the spilling of blood in murder is somehow analogous to the spilling of blood in the loss of virginity.

The vision of life and death as a continuum that is established in the play engenders a sense of history without needing to be as specific as the choruses in Greek tragedy. The opening chorus in the *Agamemnon* gives names, places, and events as a way of constructing a tradition of bloodshed that gives an ominous prescience of the action to come. There it is a matter of the race, the tribe. For Lorca too it becomes not only a national question and a class question, but a question of the species as a whole. The price paid for this widened scope is of course a ritualization of the action to the point where it is so predestined as to be slightly rigid. Another way of saying this would be that destiny does not issue from character as in Greek drama, but rather from some outside source, some pattern larger than life itself. For all that, the lyric insets coupled with the cyclic nature of time in the play make for a very powerful equivalent of the choric purpose. Furthermore, it avoids the practical problems of staging that Eliot had to cope with. Lorca's rural poor are more convincing than the slightly literary poor of Canterbury, at the same time that they are closer to the class that gave birth to the dithyramb so long ago in Athens. They partake of the eternal elements of agricultural life, which by and large change less than do the elements of the city in a similar stretch of time. Eliot's stage dialogue, too, is full of theological and historical problems of a complexity somewhat too distant from the simplicity of the choric odes, while in *Bodas de Sangre* there is a harmony of all the parts of the play, a continuous toughness and economy unbroken by long speeches or intellectual elaboration. One cannot help but sense that this is somehow closer to the feeling of early tragedy, while at the same time contributing a strong modernizing technique which aids in keeping the tradition alive and potent in the twentieth century.

It seems that there must have been some sort of musical accompaniment for the Greek choruses. Certainly, the songs in Shakespeare must have been backed by at least a viol. There is no reason why music could not be used in a similar capacity in modern plays. Nietzsche, after all, postulated that tragedy itself was born out of the spirit of music, and his model in his own time, Wagner, had very well-developed ideas about the subject. He found a choric equivalent in the orchestra, on whose continuous flow the voices of the singers were to ride like boats on the water. The inclusion of songs in the text of a play, though not so sweeping a revision of the tradition as Wagner proposed, could still have several advantages over other forms of choric expression.

In *Mutter Courage und ihre Kinder* (1939), Bertolt Brecht employs this scheme using original songs in the popular idiom. Clearly, the initial problem is that the music is bound to be anachronistic in one way or another. Although the play is set in the seventeenth century, songs in the idiom of that time would deprive the play of immediacy, and contemporary songs would mar the historical illusion. Brecht's choice of a modern idiom is, however, the only possible one, since he never uses historical material for its own sake so much as for its impact on the present. The songs he uses increase our sympathy for the characters, at the risk of overpopularizing into a kind of Marxist musical comedy. As it is, the songs enjoy the same sort of narrow escape from preciousness as the plays do from didacticism. In the latter case, we are given the conflict between a debased world and the unspoken solutions to its problems. In the case of the songs, we are given poignant or unnerving lyrics that seem to be in conflict with their own rhythmic and metrical schemes. The result has a little of the *double entendre* of Blake's *Songs of Innocence and Experience*, or of Goethe's *Faust*. Sometimes the songs are satirical, depending upon the lighthearted expression of dismal or repugnant sentiments. A short example is the soldier's song in the sixth part:

> Ein schnaps, Wirt, schnell, sei g'scheit!
> Ein Reiter hat kein Zeit.
> Muss für sein Kaiser streiten.
>
> . . . .

Dein Brust, Weib, schnell, sei g'scheit!
Ein Reiter hat kein Zeit.
Er muss gen Mähren reiten.

. . . .

Trumpf aus, Kamerad, sei g'scheit!
Ein Reiter hat kein Zeit.
Muss kommen, solang sie werben.

Dein Spruch, Pfaff, schnell, sei g'scheit!
Ein Reiter hat kein Zeit.
Er muss fürn Kaiser sterben (p. 1402).[4]

(A schnaps, host, quick, be clever!
A trooper has no time.
Must fight for his Kaiser.

. . . .

Your breast, woman, quick, be clever!
A trooper has no time.
He must go ride horses.

. . . .

Play trumps, comrade, be clever!
A trooper has no time.
Must come as long as they recruit.

Your text, parson, quick, be clever!
A trooper has no time.
He must die for his Kaiser.)

Here, in the rhetoric of a German beer-drinking song,
the soldier expresses two fundamental elements of the
choric stance. First, there is a desire to embrace the

[4] Bertholt Brecht, *Gesammelte Werke*, 4[er] band, Frankfurt
am Main, 1967.

pleasures of life with gusto. This is of course undercut by the vulgarity with which he treats woman in the same breath as wine and cards, yet what follows vindicates it in part. Second, there is the sense of brevity of life that makes immediacy necessary. So, too, our attitude towards the singer is divided. We see him first as frivolous and self-indulgent, then we are given a second look which makes him more sympathetic. He is a man whose life is not his own, and whose vulgarity is in part due to that fact. The traditional cycle of the seasons is replaced by the unnatural but certainly just as time-honored pattern of war—live rapidly and die young. Yet there is no question of heroism. This man is nameless, just another soldier, more cannon-fodder. The lack of meaning he foresees in his death belies the supposedly noble act of dying for the Kaiser. It is at once satire, self-satire and class satire. It resonates from the specific case to a much larger condition.

The satirical song in Brecht is ordinarily fraught with a kind of cynicism that causes, in this order, contempt and pity for the speaker. There are other songs, however, which win us to the characters in less oblique ways. Consider, for example, the song which occupies the entirety of part ten:

Uns hat eine Ros ergetzet
Im Garten mittenan
Die hat sehr schön geblühet
Haben sie im März gesetzet
Und nicht umsonst gemühet.
Wohl denen, die ein Garten han
Sie hat so schön geblühet.

Und wenn die Schneewind wehen
Und blasen durch den Tann
Es kann uns wenig g'schehen
Wir habens Dach gerichtet
Mit Moos und Stroh verdichtet.
Wohl denen, die ein Dach jetzt han
Wenn solche Schneewind wehen (p. 1429).

(A rose delighted us
In the middle of the garden;
It bloomed so beautifully;
It planted in March
And did not trouble in vain.
Well for them who have a garden
That has bloomed so beautifully.

And if the snow wind blows
And through the forest blasts
It can hurt us very little;
We have a roof
Caulked with moss and straw.
Well for them who have a roof now
When such a snow wind blows.)

The choric song, we have said earlier, is always the song of home. It is the song of comfort and stability in a heroic or pseudo-heroic world of commitment to the outlands and faraway struggles of the world. Mother Courage and her last child, Kattrin, are rootless and poor, hardly heroic, although Kattrin will soon become so. She will be martyred in the next section of the play, when she tries to warn a village of an attack coming in the night. The song she hears is a last hope of security. She does not have a choice, in the sense that Achilles did, between the world of shelter and the world of risk, yet her existence in the latter world is made more touching, her sacrifice more powerful and moving, by virtue of this one last hymn of normalcy. The effect of this chorus in the play is something like the effect of Orestes' last words to Pylades before killing his mother, the one hesitation that makes the most outrageous, terrible acts *human*, comprehensible to the audience of the tragedy as well as to the characters. It makes the reader or viewer realize, suddenly, that almost all the action of the play has taken place outdoors, that shelter has been the omnipresent, but least mentioned, deprivation of the stage-figures. Just as Brecht never overtly mentions whatever political assuagements he may have in mind for a world as corrupt and destructive as the world in *Mutter Courage*, so too he never mentions, save in this brief song, the hope of peace that may —must—underlie this life of conflict. It rushes in, suddenly, close to the end, making more explicit the heartbreak and loss which the main characters have taken so stoically for the duration of the play. "Mutter Courage und Kattrin haben eingehalten, um zuzuhören, und ziehen dann weiter" (p. 1429). ("Mother Courage and Kattrin have stopped to listen, and then pull off again.")

There is an added advantage to the musical choric equivalent, which is that it is more believable to have people singing in unison than speaking in unison. Certain of Brecht's songs are so contagious that the audiences find themselves singing along. This is particularly true of *Die Dreigroschenoper*, some of whose songs have even become popular outside the play. The technique is still workable today, and has been adopted by playwrights like Peter Weiss in his *Marat-Sade*. As long as a popular idiom is used, the song-chorus will never be able to duplicate the complexity of an Aeschylean choric ode. To compensate, however, it wields irony, humor, and immediacy. Its implicit participatory aspects foreshadow more recent developments in the drama.

These three examples from the thirties certainly do not exhaust the options that have been tried. Sometimes certain rhetorical patterns, repeated phrases that occur as motifs throughout a play, can give a summarizing, refrain quality to the action, as in Pirandello's *Così è (se vi pare)*. Yeats' plays, we have mentioned earlier, use mythology and ritualized action in a fashion comparable to Lorca's. Modifications of the direct presentation of a chorus are frequent in French drama of the thirties and forties, although Cocteau is original in his use of folk and faerytale material to gain depth and lyric distance. We could of course enumerate the many devices peculiar to the cinema—flashback replacing a recitation of temporal background, as in Bergman's *Wild Strawberries*; non-progressive repetition in Resnais' *L'Année dernière à Marienbad*; or the general use of musical score to reinforce emotional crises. The superior narrative potential of the cinema—its epic proportions—have forced theatre into ceaseless exploration, into various attempts to redefine its essence. One of these has been the attempt to involve the audience directly in the play as an unmediated chorus, to reach directly to the nameless and collective rather than representing them.

The problem here is that action has usually been sacrificed in the process. The stage-figures have often been reinterpreted as *provocateurs*, not in the traditional sense of actors whose creation of events triggers emotive reaction, but in the quite opposite sense of delegates of that emotional complex, who incite response not by action but by example. One exception, however, that partakes both of contemporary trends and traditional structures is an imitation of Euripides' *Bacchae* called *Dionysos in '69*. The action is a modification of the Greek play's, calculated to insure an association between the insurgency of Dionysian revelers and the contemporary libertarian movements gathered together under the general heading of "the counterculture." The tactic here is based on a compromise between audience participation and traditional passivity, just as the text itself, varying as it did from month to month, represents a middle-ground between Euripides and the director, Richard Schechner.

The play is about the temptation, resistance, and destruction of a figure, Pentheus, in his relationship to the chorus. Here it is not a question of the chorus as normative, as song of home, but of an anachronistic chorus, like Euripides', intended to create an impression of the primitive power of the mysteries which may lie at the origin of tragedy. The confrontation of Greece and America would have been forced or painfully obvious in a straight production of the *Bacchae*, or, on the other hand, in a completely free imitation. As it is, large portions of the Greek text in translation are included in the play, surrounded by material either half-improvised or formally restructured from time to time during the play's run.

This material, seeming spontaneous, made the translated portions seem surprisingly apt, more applicable to the present than would have seemed possible.

But an additional sophistication, which makes the production worthy of mention, is the relationship of the actors to the chorus. All the members of the cast, except the person playing Pentheus, are at various times on any given night members of the chorus, regardless of what other role they may be assigned. Actors are first identified by their real names. This starts them in the same position as the audience, on the same level. Then they announce the character they will be playing, always announcing that they will have that role *that night*. This provides the conditional identification of ritual. Throughout the play, this provisional assignment of roles is refreshed from time to time by an intermingling of attributions from Euripides with biographical material from the life of the actor. A member of the audience is thus able to sympathize to a greater extent with the process by which one becomes a tragic figure. Likewise, since these same actors are also chorus members, the audience is able to feel what it means to slough off individuation and become part of a collective body. The chorus, often naked, performs rituals associated with fundamental human moments—birth, love, death—which are at the same time the moments associated by Euripides with the proto-chorus of Bacchic celebrants.

Audience participation is limited in that spectators are not encouraged to enter into the action. They are, however, drawn into the choric or reactive portions of the drama by a fairly free physical interaction between chorus members and the audience in the tiers of seats.

The architectural setup of the theatre is designed to contribute to a sense of inclusion. There are various levels encircling the central arena. An altar, supposed to reduplicate the main altar in the city Dionysia, is in close enough proximity that, in some early performances, spectators were spattered with "blood" from the sacrifices. Seeing the play was an uncomfortable experience, since the threat of involvement, voluntary or involuntary, was constantly re-invoked. Emotional reactions to Pentheus and Dionysos were sometimes overtly expressed, and to one extent or another the viewer was forced to recapitulate the choice of the hero, Pentheus, as he vacillates between principle and fascination. This sense of involvement, since it remains potential and hence orderly, does not interfere with the form of the action, and the production does not degenerate into unliterary anarchy. Even when, as was the case in some performances, the audience spilled out into the street following Dionysos, the effect was only that of a coda to an already realized structure.[5]

The function of the chorus, as I have tried to suggest, is a flexible one. It varies greatly from play to play in the Greek corpus, and should be expected to vary even more at the present time, when there is no one predominant type of tragedy, nor any geographical or cultural center for it. When it is not present, however, a play may be considered a tragedy only in a very dry and intellectual way. The debate about Arthur Miller's *The Death of a Salesman* centered on questions of action and social elevation of the protagonist, but the true shortcoming of the play as a tragedy—although not necessarily as a drama—

[5] Richard Schechner, *Dionysos in '69*, New York, 1970.

lay in its lack of transpersonal reference. Although we might generalize from Willy Loman to all those who suffer from similar social illusions, there was no emotional necessity to do so arising from the construction of the play itself. The distance between the aspirations of the hero and the domestic alternative to it was slight. The weakness of individuation did not serve to reinforce emotional generalization, but instead made a compromise which is quite alien to tragedy. It is as if Achilles found a middle-ground. Another way of putting it would be to say that the play simply lacks extremes of any kind. What makes it untragic is not only the pervasive sense of mediocrity but also the limitation of visionary challenge to that mediocrity.

This is not to say, of course, that we need to bring wreathed Dionysos back onto the boards, although *Dionysos in '69* shows that this possibility is not to be dismissed. The various choric equivalents that have been tried in this century have a common aim—balance, and the opposition that term implies. For just as genuine tragedy never shows us loss without compensation, so too it never shows heroism without the source—and alternative—of that heroism. Mankind is numerous, both across space and across time. That rarest of human creatures, a tragic hero, is at once a delegate from and rebel against that multiplicity. He is not superhuman, but human in some exceptional way. To show him alone, as if he had arrived at his radical position *ex nihilo*, is necessarily to diminish his relationship with the audience that perceives him. Then all we have is a literary sort of freak show. The choric part of tragedy is the part that fills in the gap between extremes, and holds them in the kind of tension that binds—and separates—the earth and the moon. I have been told that in present-day performances of Greek plays in provincial Greece, there is still a constant, shouting debate among members of the audience over questions like Orestes' matricide. The lack that we feel in Racine, for example, arises from the fact that he wrote for audiences held fast in the reserve of courtly decorum. The choric equivalent bridges the gap between actor and viewer by universalization, in a very general sense. Athens could show it in a direct and physical way. We have to be endlessly inventive.

7 The Other Tragedy

A "conflict" theory of tragedy necessarily places tragic action between optimism and pessimism, just as it finds tragic values beyond ideas of good and evil. As an empirical model, it is useful on two counts: first, that it helps to order the material of the past into an informally coherent "tradition"; and second, that it equips a critic to evaluate new material in terms of that "tradition." It is in this second function that conflict theories seem to be deficient. For if they demand compensation for loss and retribution for gain, in order to seek an explanation for at least the emotional paradox of tragedy, they are out of touch with the general pessimism that has characterized serious literature for the past century. We seem to have a kind of action, of which Beckett's is only the most recent example, that is derived less from conflict than from decline. Or, to put it another way, it is a conflict in which one of the poles is entropy or nothingness, and the other is mere existence. The trans-ethical nature of a conflict of good with good is replaced by a negation of all ethics, eventually of all value. If this were entirely a contemporary development, we could dismiss it as another manifestation of the death of tragedy in our times, or else think of it as outside tragedy altogether. This is not sufficient, however, because it does have a tradition of its own, and is derived from an alternative strain of theory of tragedy which may very well be in the ascendancy at the present time.

It is possible to give this other tragedy an ancestry stemming from Chaucer's *Monk's Tale*, which consists of several miniature non-dramatic examples of tragic action:

> Tragedie is to seyn a certeyn storie,
> As olde bookes maken us memorie,
> Of hym that stood in greet prosperitee,
> And is yfallen out of heigh degree
> Into myserie, and endeth wrecchedly.
> And they ben versified communely
> Of six feet, which men clepen *exametron*.
> In prose eek been endited many oon,
> And eek in meetre, in many a sondry wyse.[1]

The action in question is simply that of a fall, perhaps coming to Chaucer through a trans-latinate rumor of Aristotle, but more likely influenced by the *Consolation of Philosophy* of Boethius. Every fall of the sort called tragic by Chaucer is caused by an espousal of Fortuna, or earthly hopes, instead of divine hope. Fortune is seen as a wheel, an emblem of change. He who gives it his allegiance is first carried high, and then brought low. The criterion that Chaucer uses in the choice of his examples is simple: the hero must be famous. It is understood that there is a homiletic generalization to be applied to people of any stature. Along with characters from classical tragedies, Chaucer includes, somewhat disarmingly, Adam, Sampson, and Lucifer. In the Boethian tradition, what these heroes ought to have done was to turn away from the allures of the temporal world and commit themselves

---

[1] Chaucer, Geoffrey, *The Works of Geoffrey Chaucer*, ed. F. Robinson, Boston, 1957, p. 189.

to a transcendental world that is unchanging. Tragedy
then becomes synonymous with the catastrophic waste
of human life and esperance.

Although this elegant and simple conception of tragedy
may very well be present in Shakespeare, still it does not
enter into the practice of tragedy until the nineteenth
century, where its source is not Chaucer but Schopenhauer in *Die Welt als Wille und Vorstellung* (1, #51 and
II, #37).[2] Like Hegel, Schopenhauer has the highest opinion of tragedy: "Als der Gipfel der Dichtkunst sowohl
in Hinsicht auf die Grösste der Wirkung als auf die
Schwierigkeit der Leistung ist das Trauerspiel anzusehn
und ist dafür anerkannt" (I, p. 353). ("Tragedy must be
regarded and recognized as the apex of poetic art both in
regard to the magnitude of the effect and the difficulty
of achievement.") Where Hegel found in tragic action
a self-contradiction of the Absolute—this is the source
of many "conflict" theories—Schopenhauer found it to
be, similarly, "der Widerstreit des Willens mit sich selbst"
(I, p. 353). ("The conflict of the Will with itself.") But
this is as far as the resemblance goes. For where Hegel
found in tragedy all the inevitability that any embodiment of the Absolute must have, Schopenhauer saw it as
the

> Leiden der Menschheit . . . welches nun herbeigeführt
> wird teils durch Zufall und Irrtum, die als Beherrscher
> der Welt, und durch ihre bis zum Schein der Absicht-
> lichkeit gehende Tücke als Schicksal personifiziert,
> auftreten . . . (I, p. 353).

[2] Schopenhauer, Arthur, *Sämtliche Werke*, ed. Wolfgang
Frhr. von Löhneysen, Stuttgart, 1960.

(suffering of mankind . . . which is produced in part
through chance and error, which appear to be the rul-
ers of the world, and which through their appearance
of intention and their malice are personified as fate. . . .)

When we understand that Schopenhauer means by
"will" nothing more or less than a pernicious version of
what Hegel means by "Absolute," it should then be apparent that it is not so much a literary as a philosophical
divergence that separates them. For the "substance" of
the Absolute that Hegel sees in tragic heroes, the unde-
finable, other-worldly quality that gives them their size
and nobility, is for Schopenhauer a curse that renders
them mere negative examples. For Schopenhauer, this
quality is only egotism, a burden as great as the body, perhaps one and the same. Yet what makes them truly heroic,
and what makes tragedy the most prestigious form of art,
is their ultimate turning away from the vicious goals and
cross-purposes of tragic action toward "das Aufgeben
nicht bloss des Lebens, sondern des ganzen Willens zum
Leben selbst" (I, p. 354). ("the surrender not only of
life, but of the entire will to live itself.") There is no sense
of compensation for loss in tragedy, since there is no
compensation for life or death in Schopenhauer's world.
Hamartia has nothing to do with a character's behavior,
nor his moral attributes. Instead, it is "die Schuld des
Daseins selbst" (I, p. 354). ("the guilt of existence itself.") Not only are the characters witnessed in their
turning away from life; the audience itself must experience resignation, a strange variation on *catharsis*:

Im Augenblick der tragischen Katastrophe wird und
deutlicher als jemals die Überzeugung, dass das Leben

ein schwerer Traum sei, aus dem wir zu erwachen haben (II, p. 556).

(In the moment of tragic catastrophe, the conviction comes to us more clearly than ever that life is a bad dream from which we must awaken.)

Few critics would give this account much credence as a description of tragedy. Few would allow it even suggestiveness. In the first place, there is little empirical ground for what it says. This even Schopenhauer admits. "Ich räume ein, dass im Trauerspiel der Alten dieser Geist der Resignation selten direkt hervortritt und ausgesprochen wird" (II, p. 557). ("I concede that in ancient tragedy the spirit of resignation is seldom directly set forth and expressed.") A few examples are given, with ample—perhaps too ample—qualification. In the second place, even if audiences were by and large prepared to accept an ethical interpretation of tragedy, and there is no evidence that they are, it is doubly unlikely that they would be willing to accept the specific ethical premises that Schopenhauer promotes. Here we see, even more markedly than in Hegel, the subjugation of aesthetic judgment to the demands of a closed philosophical system. What is admirable is not so much the insight into the subject in question, but instead the deftness with which it is justified according to the model.

Interestingly, Schopenhauer is almost alone among theorists of tragedy in preferring modern to classical examples. For although the Greeks show the world under the domination of chance and error, they do not show the resignation that is to cure that condition. In Shakespeare, for example, this resignation is expressed in the digressive scenes, presumably the soliloquies. They give us a familiarity with the thought processes which must necessarily be accessible if we are to perceive so intellectual an attribute as resignation. Schopenhauer apparently finds modern tragedy more "philosophical" in the popular sense of the word. There is more overt speculation about the position of the individual in the cosmos. It is strange that he ignores the Greek choruses that would seem best to illustrate his case, such as those in *Oedipus Coloneus*. For all these inconsistencies, however, there are more than a few practitioners of the art who are familiar with his writings and are influenced by them. Some examples are in order, but before we get to them it is necessary to note that in many cases Schopenhauer does not endure in a "pure" condition. His impact on posterity is inexorably linked with that of Wagner and Nietzsche, both of whom absorbed and modified his tenets before passing them on.

Nietzsche's *Die Geburt der Tragödie* is largely a reaction against Schopenhauer, although it owes much to him, as Nietzsche himself makes clear in his self-critical introduction of 1886. Nietzsche's mind is hortatory and parabolic, never homiletic in the Schopenhauerian fashion. Nietzsche also subsumes ethics under aesthetics; Schopenhauer does quite the opposite. For all that, though, the idea of a heroism that rises from an amorphous source of energy only to be re-absorbed into it is deeply reminiscent of Schopenhauer's graceful nihilism. To relate these two philosophers, there is a need for a middle term, and that would be Wagner. The action of *Der Ring des Nibelungen* certainly belongs to the pattern of *Die Welt als Wille und Vorstellung*. The entire cosmos, of gods and mortals alike, is depicted in an intricate decline in which heroes, heroines, and villains are united in annihilation. There is much explicit Schopenhauer in the text as well, as Nietzsche points out in *Der Fall Wagner*. Wagner, who conceived of himself as the modern Aeschylus, is in fact Aeschylus only to the "other" tragedy of decline. In his hands, the action of heroism becomes a prolonged elegy. The *leitmotiv* is a device designed both to stimulate and simulate memory, so that the actions of the characters are aggrandized by music as if they were happening long ago. Repetition of a musical phrase serves to integrate the appearances of these characters over the considerable length of time involved in the four operas. There is a sense in which Nietzsche's choric ideal is borrowed from Wagner's ideas about the orchestra as an ever-flowing continuum of emotion of which the singers are only surface apparitions. The orchestra, as a body of feeling, is present, as it were, before the beginning and after the end. It is less a Schopenhauerian nothingness than a kind of world-consciousness or collective unconscious.

It is likely that the aesthetic value given to the orchestra in Wagner is at least partly responsible for the aesthetic and musical character of the chorus in Nietzsche's work. The phrase *principium individuationis*, which Nietzsche borrows straight from Schopenhauer, reduces the characters to insubstantial paradigmatic beings, and this attitude in Nietzsche would have been reinforced by the Wagnerian distancing—some call it rigidity—of stage figures. It is generally true of the Schopenhauerian strain of tragedy that individual and distinctive personality traits on the part of the hero or heroine are seen as unimportant, or, worse yet, pathetic attempts to maintain singular existence in a general entropy. When Brunhilde rides onto the funeral pyre at the close of *Götterdämmerung*, we are dealing with the demise of an archetype, not the death of a human being. It is this aspect of Schopenhauer that infects Nietzsche's Apollonians, that makes them seem static objects of contemplation. When we speak of a tradition of tragedy coming from Schopenhauer, it is really this curious admixture of three minds that we mean. Many modern playwrights who claim to be influenced by Nietzsche read much like Schopenhauer, and it is not easy to sort out the skeins.

At the risk of violating chronology, it is best to begin with a fairly simple dramatic example of this tradition. In Chekhov's *Uncle Vanya*, Voinitsky says: "When people have no real life, they live on their illusions. Anyway, it's better than nothing" (p. 209).[3] Members of the leisure class, people who have every reason to find life rewarding, they are always in the country on isolated estates. Boredom, which Dostoevsky called an aristocratic sensation, is their greatest enemy. The "action" of the play consists in nothing more than the revelation of their emptiness. By contrast we are given more active characters, like Astrov, the doctor. Occupied both as a forester and a medical practitioner, he too can only lament: "I work harder than anyone in the district . . . but there's no small light in the distance. I'm not expecting anything for myself any longer" (p. 211). There is a choice, then, like that which Schopenhauer expresses at the end of his

---

[3] Chekhov, Anton, *Plays*, trans. Elisaveta Fen, Harmondsworth, 1959.

first volume. Either we indulge the will, or we suppress it: the result is the same—nothingness.

Entropy is not limited to the human world. Just as the characters are always remarking to one another that they have lost their looks, or lack their former energy, so too the natural world seems doomed:

> [Astrov] Now look at this. It's a map of our district as it was fifty years ago; half of the whole area was covered with forest . . . elks and wild goats were common. . . . This lake was the home of swans, geese and ducks. . . . Cattle and horses were numerous. . . . Now let us look lower down. This is how it was twenty-five years ago. Already only a third of the area is under forest. The goats have disappeared, but there are still some elks. . . . Now look at the third section, the map showing the district as it is now. . . . The elks, swans and woodgrouse have all disappeared. There's not a trace of the small farms and monasteries and mills that were there before. [. . .] In general, it's an unmistakable picture of gradual decay which will obviously be completed in another ten or fifteen years. You may say that it is the influence of civilization (p. 222).

Civilization, or culture, has become an instrument of death, and its upholder in the play, the professor Serebriakov, is an aesthetician who, according to general estimates, knows nothing about art. In his self-proclaimed wisdom, he has been above management of the estate, and has demanded prolonged sacrifices from Sonia and Uncle Vanya, daughter and brother-in-law by an earlier marriage. Proclaiming humanistic abstraction, he is wholly inhuman with respect to living people. What conflict there is in the play is between this man and Uncle Vanya.

But Voinitsky's rebellion against the man who has exploited him does not change him. When he drives the professor and his entourage away, the sense of emptiness only redescends on the house. What alternative order, after all, could Vanya offer to the hypocrisy and vacuousness of his adversary? He speaks of past ambitions: "If I had had a normal life, I might have been a Schopenhauer . . ." (p. 231). In other words, he might have been able to make something, at least a book, out of his despair. But when the battle is over, no one is destroyed, nothing is changed, nothing is re-ordered. They have fought like rats under shock in the behaviorist's box. "We must go on living!" Sonia concludes, "We shall live through a long, long succession of days and tedious evenings. . . . When the time comes we shall die submissively . . ." (p. 245).

Chekhov called two of his darkest plays, *The Seagull* and *The Cherry Orchard*, "comedies." Certainly, there is in each of them an abundance of local ironies and amusing exchanges, yet the overall darkness more than nullifies whatever positive counterthrust laughter might give. Even *Uncle Vanya* is not called a tragedy, but rather is subtitled "Scenes from Country Life." Perhaps Chekhov was aware of the divergence of his drama from the mainstream of the tragic tradition, or perhaps, as his temperament would indicate, he was not willing to admit the catastrophic implications of his own work. Schopenhauer said that comedy is the opposite of tragedy, and this is clearly nonsense. Indeed, the more the problem is examined, the more difficult it becomes to distinguish economically between the two. In general, it can be said that comedy is also a drama of conflict, but that it differs from tragedy in that the demands of the opposing sides are negotiable, where they can never be in tragedy. The conflict in all of Chekhov, as in all Schopenhauerian tragedy, is between being and nothingness, with nothingness always victorious. In a sense this typical situation exists outside considerations of negotiability, since death "solves" every confrontation sooner or later, and resignation is merely surrender, after all.

The laughter in Chekhov, then, is always hollow or else hysterical. It expresses not control but its opposite, at best a momentary distraction. The plays all fulfill Schopenhauer's main prescription for tragedy, that they direct the audience or reader toward an attitude of resignation. At the close of *Uncle Vanya*, for example, there is nothing to be found in life except the expectation that rest shall follow it, that the will shall somehow cease forcing the characters to experience hope and desire. The characters themselves wish to divest themselves of the *principium individuationis*. They are looking for a choric impulse which the world no longer affords them. The "other tragedy" postulates that consciousness itself is an act of rebellion sufficient to bring on retribution and suffering.

Thomas Mann's *Der Tod in Venedig* is an excellent illustration of the admixture of Schopenhauerian and Nietzschean influences. The artist, and in particular the tragic artist, has for Schopenhauer the ability to foster the kind of resignation that allows respite from the hungering of the will. In a much later essay on Schopenhauer, Mann writes: "Der Künstler als Vorstufe des über den Willen zum Leben überhaupt hinausgekommenen *Heiligen*—das ist Schopenhauer" (p. 76).[4] ("The artist as a stage toward a sainthood free of the will to live—that is Schopenhauer.") This ascetic ideal is embodied by Aschenbach, who for his art "hatte . . . das Gefühl gezügelt und erkältet" (p. 449).[5] ("Had bridled and cooled his sensibility.") He is the author of a novel with the Schopenhauerian title *Maja*, a word used in *Die Welt als Wille und Vorstellung* to refer to the transient and insidious deceptions of the phenomenal world. Willing in his youth to give up everything to art, Aschenbach has become something of an official writer. He has strayed from the passive heroism of his early characters; his head has been turned with honors. At the very beginning of the tale we already see his "will-lessness" crumbling. His desire to travel—which can only be a desire for bodily movement—is the primary symptom.

On the boat to Venice, Aschenbach sees an old man among a group of youthful revelers. He is marked with all the hideous physical deteriorations of old age, yet he behaves with all the equally hideous bravado of the young. This man, who foreshadows some of the changes that will befall Aschenbach, is on the one hand a figure embodying the mindless physicality of the will, and on the other hand is obviously intended as a sort of Silenus figure. He is referred to at one point as "Ziegenbart," or "goat-beard" (p. 461), a sobriquet suggestive of conventional Dionysian imagery. From this point on, what happens in the story is at once a rising of the will, in Schopenhauer's terms, and a revenge of the Dionysian in

[4] Mann, Thomas, *Schopenhauer*, Stockholm, 1938.
[5] Mann, Thomas, *Gesammelte Werke*, 8er band, Berlin, 1960.

Nietzschean terms. There is no way to separate these two philosophical skeins wrapped around the *Novelle*. This piece of Hellenic myth is followed by another. The boatman, an outlaw gondolier, whom Aschenbach has hired to take him to the steamship landing is quite clearly the ferryman Charon:

> Selbst wenn du es auf meine Barschaft abgesehen hast und mich hinterrücks mit einen Ruderschlage ins Haus des Aides schickst, wirst du mich gut gefahren haben (p. 466).

> (Even if you have seen my cash and send me down into the house of Hades with an oar, still you have driven me well.)

A blissful sense of forgetfulness comes over Aschenbach, as if he really were crossing the Styx.

The fundamental dialectic of the tale is expressed as follows:

> Einsamkeit zeitigt das Originale, das gewagt und befremdend Schöne, das Gedicht. Einsamkeit zeitigt aber auch das Verkehrte, das Unverhältnismässige, das Absurde und Unerlaubte (p. 468).

> (Solitude begets the original, the risky and unfamiliar beauty, begets poetry. But solitude also begets the perverse, the disproportionate, the absurd and illicit.)

It is as if both sides of Aschenbach, which had been suppressed for years in their essential intensity, are about to reassert themselves in direct ways and destroy him. The epiphany of the aging reveler is followed closely by the first vision of Tadzio. Noticing the boy's perfect beauty, he finds him "von holdem und göttlichen Ernst" ("of sweet and godlike seriousness"), and is reminded "an griechische Bildwerke aus edelster Zeit" (p. 469) ("of the noblest time in Greek artwork"). The boy resembles Apollo. In Nietzsche's terms, the Apollonian is associated with serene sculpted heads such as those found on the Parthenon, a beauty of an elevated and detached nature. Apollo also has a special significance for Schopenhauer, as Mann himself points out in his essay:

> Apollon, der Fernhintreffende, der Musengott, ist ein Gott der Ferne und der Distanz,—nicht des Verstrickt-seins, des Pathos und der Pathologie,—des Leidens nicht, sondern der Freiheit, ein objektiver Gott, der Gott der Ironie. In Ironie also, so sah es Schopen-hauer, in der genialen Objektivität, war die Erkenntnis dem Sklavendienste des Willens entrissen, die Auf-merksamkeit länger von kleinem Motiv des Wollens getrübt: wir waren im Zustande einer Hingebung . . . (pp. 33-34).

> (Apollo, the far-shooter, God of the Muses, is a God of distance and space—not of pain, pathos and pathol-ogy—not of suffering, but of freedom, an objective God, the God of irony. Thus in irony, according to Schopenhauer, in ingenious objectivity, knowledge was loosed from its slavery to the will, and attention no longer blurred by petty purpose of desire: we were in a state of resignation . . .).

Tadzio becomes an emblem of the pure, ironic detach-ment which is the characteristic of genuine art. It is ironic also because it is precisely this ideal from which Aschenbach has strayed in his love of worldly honor. He is thus taunted with his own failure at the same time that he is prey to recurrent assertions of the will, of physicality, of precisely that pathos and disease of which the boy is the antithesis.

The ideal, then, of a purely representational beauty outside the sphere of the will is presented to the protagonist. Yet he is in the grip of the will and reacts to the revelation wrongly. He sees the boy's head not as that of Apollo, but as "das Haupt des Eros" (p. 474) ("the head of Eros"). He is not disinterested, but quite the opposite. His admiration quickly degenerates into Purpose. He spends his days designing ways to place himself in proximity to Tadzio. Recapitulating the Silenus figure on the boat, he goes to a hairdresser who makes up his face in the image of youth. Disease runs wild in the city, and analogous disease assails him: "Der Alternde die Ernüchterung nicht wollte. . . . Der Rausch ihm zer teuer war" (p. 494). ("The aging man did not want the cure. . . . His intoxication was too dear to him.") Finally a dreadful Dionysian vision of violence and revelry comes to him in a dream, and he sees through the illusion of the *principium individuationis*, sees the terrible energy of the will to live.

As a blend of Schopenhauerian and Nietzschean tragedy, *Der Tod in Venedig* possesses both conflict and decline as vital elements in its construction. The decline is obvious enough, not in the repetitive manner in which it takes place in Chekhov, but through a graphic account of the disintegration of a single human being. The conflict may be interpreted in either of two ways. On the one hand it is the conflict from *Die Geburt der Tragödie*, where an image of Apollonian form rises from an ever-intensifying mass of Dionysian energy. Aschenbach, in this interpretation, dies because he is spiritually torn in half. The compromises by which he lived are taken from him. The contrary demands of the two forces which are released upon him with unprecedented power are, like all tragic polarities, non-negotiable, not open to solution by compromise. On the other hand, it is possible to see the conflict as a confrontation of the world as will and the world as representation. Aschenbach sees, as he has not seen since his youth, if he saw it then, an image of the world of mind or ideas which is not subject to the will. It is the world of art, which in its ideal disinterest negates the purposiveness of the will for a while at least, and suggests a higher mode of existence that might be called resignation. Yet he is unable to attain to this level. He approaches what ought to be beyond motivation with interest and design. He gives himself over to the sway of the will, which revenges itself upon him with its own series of visions, and which ultimately destroys him while the boy, the delegate of Apollo, the God of irony, appears before his darkening eyes on the sand, beckoning.

What makes Mann's hybrid *feel* more like a traditional tragedy is its complete presentation of an alternative, so that there is at least a possibility of choice on the part of the protagonist. The protagonist in this instance is weak, however, and prefers to let fate, or what Schopenhauer would call chance and error, take over for volition. Furthermore, even if there were a choice it would resemble the Achilles' choice of tragic convention very slightly. The hero in the "other" tragedy is as much a victim as a hero. Certainly we feel that this is true for Chekhov's people, and for Aschenbach as well. There is no compensation, no balance. We are simply witnesses to the dismemberment of a spirit that does not fight back. The only fully realized order that these protagonists carry with them into the situation is existence, consciousness. It is a reductionism of sweeping consequences. At its best it produces a moving account of human failure. At its worst, however, it is sheer nihilism, as in the case of its most influential recent practitioner, Samuel Beckett.

Local humor is much more effective in Beckett than in Chekhov, and many readers and audiences react to him as a comedian. This would seem to belie the influence of Schopenhauer, whom Beckett read as early as 1930,[6] since comedy for that philosopher is a deception, a lying drop of the curtain at the exact moment of reconciliation and good cheer, never showing the inevitable suffering and death that would follow were the play to continue long enough. Yet there is no reason to assume an identity of humor and comedy. Schopenhauer, in his partisanship of modern tragedy, nowhere decries Shakespearean humor. There does exist, however, a moment now and again in Beckett where an affirmation, however minute, can be ascertained. Against the environment of total entropy, this moment can seem much more important than its intrinsic content. The question that must be asked is whether or not this characteristic of Beckett's work is sufficiently important to play a part in an evaluation of his work in terms of either tragic tradition.

In *Watt*, which was written in the Unoccupied Zone in France during World War II and published in 1953, the protagonist is a compulsive little man who obtains a

[6] Janvier, Ludovic, *Beckett par lui-même*, Paris, 1969, p. 12.

position as servant at the house of a man named Knott. The master, like a castle official in Kafka, is rarely seen. He never goes forth from the house, never entertains guests, and never communicates directly with his employees. All the procedures necessary to the maintenance of the mansion are ritualized to the point of automation, and Watt, perfect for the situation, worries every minor problem out to pages of intense but pointless reasoning and enumeration. The book, like a fair part of Beckett's other work, seems to be about the reduction of mankind by routine, and by the seeming necessity of work. Both master and servant seem to be enslaved by some unseen force, just as the jewels in a watch are subservient to some other principle of which they may very well be unaware. Needless to say, no hint of a higher principle exists in Beckett, however. Watt's main deviation from his inane duties consists in an occasional meeting with a servant from another house in the shared garden area outside. There develops one of those half-friendship, half-homosexual relationships that recur in Beckett's work in Didi and Gogo or Hamm and Clov. This second person assumes some of the narration of the novel. He speaks of his relationship with Watt, and how in fact they have met only very infrequently. On one occasion, after they have paced up and down together for a space, he says: "To be together again, after so long, who love the sunny wind, the windy sun, in the sun, in the wind, that is perhaps something, perhaps something."[7]

Now of course it is silly to assume that such a minute fleck of light in the constant nothingness of the book is in any way strong enough to create a balance. But it is

[7] Beckett, Samuel, *Watt*, New York, 1959, p. 163.

an unusual deviation from the routine of anticipated disaster. Similar instances occur in the plays. In the broken-record dialogue of *Waiting for Godot*, where a breakdown of memory, emotion, and consciousness itself seems to accompany every further deterioration of the physique, at least occasional impulses of self-justification remain: "We have kept our appointment and that's an end to that. We are not saints, but we have kept our appointment. How many people can boast as much?"[8] Or we could cite the persistence of compassion as a value in *Endgame*:

Clov: Why do I always obey you? Can you explain that to me?

Hamm: No. . . . Perhaps it's compassion.
        (pause)
        A kind of great compassion.
        (pause)
        Oh you won't find it easy, you won't find it easy.[9]

But the impression persists that such rays of light are deliberately set up by the author as clay pigeons. For to depict despair, is it not vital to show the last flickering of hope? The moments of peace and gratitude are transient: they do not leave, as in, say, Proust, the foundations of an available system of redemption. Nor are they numerous or substantial enough to offset the pessimism to any significant extent.

In Schopenhauerian tragedy, the reigning and proper

[8] Beckett, Samuel, *Waiting for Godot*, New York, 1954, p. 51.

[9] Beckett, Samuel, *Endgame*, New York, 1958, p. 76.

order of the world is silence, and any human achievement or ambition is a disorder that will be purged regardless of the means taken to uphold it. This is a far cry from the clash of orders in the *Oresteia*, not only because meaningful synthesis is out of the question, but also, again, because it is so devastating a reduction. Even if we were to allow isolated moments of contentment, humor or respite from pain in a work, would that be enough to make a claim for compensation? It may be that we are approaching a time when only Schopenhauerian tragedy will be comprehensible, where any heroism resembling the tradition will be regarded as naive and humorless, where Apollo is incredible and Dionysos jaded. Perhaps this tendency may be traced to the increasing abstraction visible in Kleist and Melville, where instead of making an absolute identification with the state, the family or some other socio-ethical category, the hero identifies mainly with absoluteness itself. What makes Antigone greater than her individual self is now directed toward the intensification of self. Instead of "transcending out" one "transcends in." In Chekhov or Beckett, however, all that remains is the hunger for a transcendental identification. By *Waiting for Godot* and *Endgame*, the characters find themselves in a condition much closer to Schopenhauer's resignation. Hope and expectation—the will— are greeted with a cold eye, although they keep involuntarily asserting themselves.

We may ask of Beckett, and of Schopenhauer, why they have taken the trouble to write, assuming that they believe in the general vanity of human endeavor as they say. In Schopenhauer's case, the justification comes from the value placed on art, and there must have been a sense in which he regarded his system as an aesthetic object. For Beckett as well, there is an occasional positive value associated with narration. In *Malone Dies*, an old man past hope of recovery must pass the time until, mercifully, actual death comes to relieve the living death in which he finds himself. In order to fill the days, he makes up stories, miserable defeated tales of unintelligent youths and incompetent, self-deluding adults. In the Schopenhauer tradition, he is scrupulously truthful, trying not to disguise the condition of the world and himself. Hence his narrative is peppered with self-critical commentary, such as "What tedium!" In a parody of choric song, the figures of his stories rise and fall in and out of the voice. Although the tales of Saposcat and Macmann are pointless, issueless and bleak, there is something about their creation that is more valuable than the other activities of the dying man, compulsive counting and arranging of his own possessions in preparation for a penultimate inventory he will never make. Through the construction of the stories, we see that the mere existence of the mind is heroic, somehow intrinsically valuable, and not only in the sense of fostering resignation. In Malone the death of the imagination which Beckett predicts is not complete. There is still creation: "Yes, a little creature, I shall try and make a little creature, to hold in my arms, a little creature in my image, no matter what I say."[10] Bravely, without self-pity, the tales keep coming until death stops the pen.

Beckett's works are full of silence, like white spaces in Chinese art. These appear to be intended to let the underlying nothingness show through from time to time

[10] Beckett, Samuel, *Malone Dies*, London, 1962, p. 65.

onto the surface of the work. The "other" tragedy has absorbed many elements from mainstream tragedy and given them new emphasis. One of these elements is precisely that silence. Aristotle's *catharsis*, if the term has any meaning, would have to be located temporally at the end of the play. This is the point at which the audience must return to the world, when the *Pequod* disappears under the waves, when the last words of the play are spoken. The applause, as Rilke suggested, serves to ward off whatever it is that would make them change their lives. In traditional tragedy, this moment is charged with both terror and exhilaration, the fear of death and the joy of life. In the "other" tragedy this silence is the underpinning of all the words and actions. It is equally contradictory. It is at once the will to live and the proximity of nothingness.

It is easy to see how Schopenhauerian tragedy brings the terms somewhat closer to the popular usage. It is of course very hard to ascertain whether the change in the term or the change in the literature came first. In any case, it is a surrogate tragedy rather than an actual development, and is probably a dead end with Beckett, whose mastery of the variant is inimitable. Tragedy seeks the ideological center of its time, and in our day the whirlwind of ideologies may have created a spiritual vacuum. The even more dramatic reductionism of the most recent works of Beckett points to a self-destructive tendency in the strain. Whatever value judgments we place upon it in the light of tragic conventions, however, should not impede an overall judgment of it as literature. From this viewpoint, it has been, almost against its own designs, a fruitful and engaging species.

IIIIIIIIIIIIIIIIIIIIIIIIIIIIIIIIIIIIIIIIIIIIIIIIIIIIIIIIIIIIIIIIIIIIIII

We have arrived at a period in history when all tragedy
has become elegiac, because it celebrates an individualism
which can have meaning only in a less populous world.
Revolutionaries have replaced rebels. The *status quo* chal-
lenged by every tragic hero was first ideological, and only
later a matter of power. We live in an era when power
is primary, and is served by words only *post facto*. This
means that it is increasingly difficult for one man or
woman to raise a vision of another world order in such
a way that his or her rebellion is genuinely dangerous.
The leading symptom of this condition is a verbal one.
It is harder now than ever before to utter a real heresy,
to shock someone with words alone. Tragedy is, for better or for worse, a literary phenomenon, and never before has that term implied such distance from the social,
political, ethical, or religious governance of our lives.
Nowadays there are methods for disposing of would-be
heroes. These methods are reminiscent of Lenin's carrot
and stick. Either there is a systematic outreach that ab-
sorbs the rebel vision into the mainstream, or there is a
technocratic means of suppression. The fact that a critic
may speak generally of "tragic heroism" is a symptom
of the problem in itself, since no tragic hero ought to be
included in a group or category. There is a danger that
the study of tragedy may recede into the antiquarian
right before our eyes. Shall we accede to the usage of
newspapers and accept the idea that a plane crash is really

a tragedy, that it is now quantity and not quality that ennobles loss?

Each tragic hero, in his defeat, beats on the boundaries of existence and makes them less limiting. The limits had to come from the idea of a community, where every individual had a name and a local function. This sort of community, with a system of individual craftsmanship interlocking for the common good, this pure division of labor, is a far cry from revolutionary ideas of communality or communism. These larger economies are geared to units of such massive size that every individual must be expendable. Tragedy is a remnant of the time when no one was. The older idea of community is an organic one, and the malfunction of one member of the community analogous to the failure of an organ of the body. That "body politic" has now become the "system."

Any sensible approach to tragedy must take stock of the community in which the tragic action is placed. To study tragedy is to maintain the dignity and integrity not only of the rebel, but also of the community against which his rebellion is directed. Hegel, although he limits himself entirely to considerations of action, recognizes that the oppositions in tragedy are equal ones. The Absolute is, after all, nothing more and nothing less than the sum total of all human consciousness, so that it makes a conservative assertion of community even on a metaphysical level. Antigone and Creon belong to the same world, the same community, the same family. It is precisely because there is so much that unites them that their division is shattering, overpowering. Nietzsche is even more explicit in asserting the primacy of the communal, which he calls the Dionysian. He sees it not as a disorganized revel of feeling, as we may suspect, but rather as a very ancient kind of *harmonia*. The individual or Apollonian rises from this community, and is at last re-absorbed into it. The passage of a hero is a poignant dissonance resolved by the aboriginal laws of the music that produced it.

The true father of criticism of tragedy is not, then, Aristotle, as the twentieth-century critic often assumes without question. If Aristotle does not dictate our conclusions, he does normally dictate the permissible areas of inquiry. So pervasive is his terminology that no one, including myself, is able to avoid it. The *Poetics* still provides the universe of discourse on the subject, a curious tyranny for a work so fragmented and enigmatic. So fine is its dissecting knife that the pieces it cuts cannot easily be reassembled into the whole. Nietzsche's militant generalization must be seen as a determined stand against this analysis. His attack on Socrates radiates to Aristotle in methodology. Nietzsche's work, in itself dialectical, forms an overall dialectic with Hegel's. Taken together, they generate the major paradox of tragedy: the individual in conflict with his community. I have attempted, in these essays, to employ a methodology, although a very implicit and informal one, generated by the combination of the two greatest nineteenth century writers on the subject.

If classical Greece has provided us with means of viewing tragedy, that means comes not from Aristotle but from Pythagoras. For tragedy to occur, there must be a primary organization, a community in the microcosm, a species of organization in the macrocosm. For Pythagoras this organization is numerical, but we must not equate this statement with the idea that it is purely intellectual.

"Number" in this case must be like the numbers in the first line of Keats' "Ode to Psyche." They must delineate the *harmonia* of spirit as well as thought. This harmony is to be reached only through the concord of discordant elements; there is a cosmogeny of light and dark. In tragedy we see a process by which the *harmonia* of the habitable world is restored, reaffirmed, through a contradiction. Pythagoras is said to have proven his own integrity through bilocation. Critics from Cicero to George Thomson have asserted that Aeschylus, the founder of tragedy in the form in which we have inherited it, was familiar with the works of Pythagoras. From the *Metaphysics*, we know that Aristotle was as well.

The intellectual, mathematical side of Pythagoras, the part of the mind that loves divisions, classifications, and categories, reaches us through Aristotle and Hegel. The other side, the mystical part of Pythagoras that made him a descendant of the Orphics, comes to us in Nietzsche. There is no one theorist who can give us both, yet both are indispensable to an understanding of tragedy. Certainly part of tragedy is action, and action made specific through plotting. This aspect of tragic art lends itself readily to categories and terminological distinctions. Here the influence of Aristotle is strongest, and if Hegel's scheme of tragic action resembles a Hegelian syllogism, we must allow it. The other aspect of tragic art, the irrational fervor of the community for self-preservation, escapes the Aristotelians. Nietzsche's wild leap to recover it, however crude, however maligned and discredited by classicists at the present, remains one of the most extraordinary critical acts of its century. The adrenalin injected into the tradition of criticism of tragedy by *The Birth of Tragedy* is certainly responsible, in large part, for the lavish attention given to this field in the last several decades. Pythagoras, who never saw a tragedy, stands as an ancestor of this most paradoxical of literary endeavors, of critical tasks.

Tragedy is an honorific term, there is no denying it. Applied to a recent play, it causes audiences, readers, and critics to pay more careful attention to the work. Frequently, debates over whether or not such-and-such a play is a tragedy boil down to disputes over its quality. Ideally, scholars should want to alter the term, and restrict it to a descriptive usage. Still, the number of "bad tragedies" that come to mind is small, compared with the number of "bad comedies" we could think of. It is possible that tragedy is so difficult to achieve that anything falling even slightly short of the mark must of necessity miss it altogether. In any event, most of us involuntarily cringe at the prospect of applying the machinery of tragedy to a completely ordinary human being. It is of course easier for a dramatist or novelist to depict a fall when the character is already on a height. It may take longer to convince an audience of the integrity of a humble man. No great tragedy, however, has ever asked us to accept social rank *alone* as a criterion. Many tragic heroes *are* eminently just and good, although their standard of justice may not be the same as that of the world in which they live. Likewise, what appears to that world as vice or depravity may be justice or goodness according to another code. We must conclude that a tragic hero may be drawn from any class, race, region, sex or occupation, if only he or she is outstanding or unusual in some integral way. The tragic hero is both of and against his own community of origin. Here Aristotle is misleading. He is insistent on the ethical structure of the community, but suspicious of that of the hero. This is the origin of the notion of *hamartia*.

If the hero is to contain the seeds of a new world outlook, this universality depends upon fullness of development, on the all-embracing magnitude of the new order. Every tragic hero, in his or her own way, decrees the provisional world government that Kleist's Kohlhaas does. Without this sense of size, tragedy would be no more than a gallery of misfits, monomaniacs getting their deserts from a justly outraged society. If this is true, we must discard *hamartia*, since it challenges the completeness of the protagonist's outlook, and makes an external judgment upon it. To see the hero as noble but flawed is to understand him only from the point of view of the previously established order. Suppose we allow that Kohlhaas is a man with admirable tenets about justice, who unfortunately carries his convictions too far. Is our understanding of the work enhanced by this, or have we yielded our sense of the hero's absoluteness and received nothing in return? What is, for example, the flaw of Hamlet? Is he a noble heart, a courtier *au fond* like the rest of them, whose courtly manners are marred by some fault, some *hamartia*—a tendency to overcontemplation, indecisiveness? Or is he, more properly, a delegate from another sphere of thought, a frightened advocate of persuasion (*peitho*) in an exigency of violence (*bia*)? Hamlet's apparent madness is totally logical; it seems to be insanity only when seen from the viewpoint of the king, the queen, and the antiquated laws of revenge. What seems like rationalization—the argument against killing the king while he is praying—may be an orderly cover for an inadmissible lurch of compassion. Even the deaths of Rosencrantz and Guildenstern are sad necessities like the burning of citizens' houses in *Kohlhaas*. These are contradictions, but only in terms of the conventional order, the conventional logic. What seems to be folly, overstepping the bounds of the reasonable, is really a measure of the hero's commitment to his heterocosm. It is the resolve of Achilles to remain under Troy. Aristotle's *hamartia* has been used all too often to preserve traditional notions of propriety *against those of the tragic heroes*. It is hard to see how it can be of any use to a critic or reader who desires to experience tragedy in its unadulterated power.

In fact, it is possible to assert that tragic heroes have flaws only within the confines of their own orders. For example, what undoes Kohlhaas is not so much his original resolve, with all its proclamations, as it is the abandonment of his own beliefs under pressure from an outside source. Only when he accepts the amnesty does he fall. Ahab, flawless in his own terms, succeeds utterly, with the terrible success of Lear holding dead Cordelia, of Ajax bitterly true to his deceptive vision at the end of his own sword. Like the acrophobiac who does not fall until he looks down, the tragic hero is safe within the confines of his own order. Only when he sees it from some exterior vantage point does he fall. Then Macbeth sees the moving forest, and meets the man unborn of woman.

On the subject of language, or what he calls 'thought,' Aristotle seems to stop short of the actual issue. Instead of examining the function of language in the drama, he explains the speeches in a legalistic frame of reference. "Thought," he writes, "is found where something is proved to be or not to be, or a general maxim is enunciated."[1] The proper way to approach language in tragedy, according to this, would be through rhetorical analysis. Although a great deal may be learned from this, more striking conclusions are available by way of external evaluation. Language is the barometer of stress in the world of tragedy. It is not so much a question of proofs and maxims as it is part of the general conflict. Its disruption takes the advent of disorder out of the realm of plotting alone, and places it in the very air. It is the source of all the shading and ominousness, hence is inexorably bound to the impact of a play. Allowing it the same flexibility that we gave the hero, we can affirm that it may come from any dialect, attain any degree of sophistication, or be drawn from any specialized walk of life, if only it is unusually charged within the language group from which it comes. It is a mistake, however, to see it as rational, and it is here that Nietzsche's attack on the *Poetics*, sublimated as it is into an attack on Socrates, makes the most impressive sense. For where Aristotle says, "the older poets speak the language of civic life," (pp. 63-64), we need only present the text of the *Oresteia*, with its metaphors drawn from every conceivable field of experience, as a counterexample.

The end of Aristotle's definition of tragedy in the

[1] *Aristotle's Poetics*, trans. S. H. Butcher, New York 1961, p. 64.

sixth chapter of the *Poetics* asserts that tragedy should "through pity and fear (affect) the proper purgation of these emotions" (p. 61). This passage has been subject to all sorts of exegesis. F. L. Lucas accurately classifies these interpretations as first, the religiously generated idea of purification; secondly, the one he favors, the medical practice of purgation; and third, the interpretation asserting that Aristotle meant that the passions themselves, and not their possessors, are purified. He summarizes: "In fine, 'the *catharsis* of such passions' does *not* mean that the passions are purified and ennobled, nice as that might be; it does *not* mean that men are purged of their passions; it means simply that the passions themselves are reduced to a healthy, balanced proportion."[2] Without defining any further, let us consider the moment of silence that follows the conclusion of a tragic drama, the moment of which Rilke said that the audience feels compelled to applaud in order to fend off whatever threatening presence is about to make them change their lives. It is the moment in *Moby-Dick* when the *Pequod* finally vanishes, the moment that Quentin expresses lying in his bed at Harvard and thinking about the South. To a certain extent, this sense of completion and silence exists at the end of any sequential work of art, unless it be notoriously bad or farcical. It is, among other things, the moment of greatest unity among the author, players, and audience, for the author's form is complete, the task of acting is finished, and the audience waits upon the last speeches, wondering which will contain the final words. The wordlessness between the last sentence and the applause is a special precinct, intrinsic to theatre and no other genre. Sometimes

[2] F. L. Lucas, *Tragedy*, New York 1965, p. 37.

experienced theatregoers are able to judge exactly how much silence must follow a speech for it to be the last, just as it is possible to tell that a telephone has stopped ringing by the slightest abbreviation of the last ring. Whatever Aristotle meant by *catharsis*, it is hard to think of it as anything other than an attempt to describe this moment. It is drama's most sacred point, the closing of the circle. It is moral not because it purges harmful emotions, but because it transfers the responsibility of judgment from the author to the audience, because all the evidence has been heard. It is physical not because it relates to bodily processes, but because it causes the physical participation of the spectators in applause. It is a second quintessentially present, for here the past is suddenly full and formal, and the future suddenly unsettling, full of reprisal and afterthought. It is also a moment of relief, the kind death brings to a family after a long illness in its midst.

Whether these obstacles presented to our understanding of tragedy by Aristotle are his own fault, the fault of the compilers of the *Poetics*, or the fault of centuries of commentary, it is really too late to judge. To grapple with the meaning of his categories is interesting and stimulating as a philosophical enterprise, not as a critical one. In any event, it is tangential to a serious consideration of the living tradition that tragedy presents to us. Aristotle may have had a direct influence upon the practice of tragedy in the Renaissance, but in our own century he has provoked only Brecht's reaction against him. The reverberations from other, more recent theorists are still being felt, however, and they should accordingly be given primacy in any analysis of modern tragedy. This is not to say, of course, that the *Poetics* should not continue to enhance our understanding of earlier drama. It is only to suggest that the compulsory invocation of Aristotle may be unexamined; and to point out, once again, the extremely problematical nature of his terminology, particularly as applied to literature upon which his direct impact has been limited.

Tragedy is not a genre or sub-genre; it is a pattern of literary action, action in Fergusson's sense—a "movement of spirit." This movement must then be given form. As Fergusson said, "The action which a poet first glimpses is only potentially a tragedy, until his plot-making forms it into an *actual* tragedy."[3] Tragedy is not then to be seen as a sub-philosophy or independent world view, but rather as a literary phenomenon, subject to all the laws and conventions of any genre in which it is embodied.

These statements seem obvious enough, yet they represent a minority opinion at the present time. There is a marked propensity among students and readers to apply everything directly to their lives. What would it mean to "live tragically" outside of a work of art? What would a person holding a "tragic world outlook" believe in? Was "tragedy" the prevalent ideology of ancient Greece, or was it only a favorite form of entertainment? Tragedy and life, like art in general and life, have a reciprocal relationship. Life provides the raw material. There are certain events in the world which have greater emotional power than others. The death of a man or woman before

[3] Francis Fergusson, Introduction to *Aristotle's Poetics*, trans. S. H. Butcher, New York 1961, p. 15.

his or her time is one of them. The destruction of a person acting out of a sense of principle is another. To be interested in these events is not morbid, since death inevitably gives life form, closes it, and allows its evaluation. We no longer see the slippage, the wasted energy, the false starts, or at any rate they become secondary. We *feel*, in certain lives, that there is a form. But this is an illusion, certainly, since "form" implies fixity, repeatability. Memory is insufficient to accomplish this; memory is flux, out of order, selective according to unknown laws. The role of the artist is to condense these long interstices into perceptible shapes. When we speak of a tragic event, we mean an event that resembles tragedy, that someone could make into a play or a novel, an event that has enough emotive charge to make it comparable with art.

Conversely, art moves back into life. If we have known a number of tragedies, we are more likely to see actual events in such contexts. If we have watched tragic heroes moving over pages and stages, we are prone suddenly to confuse our own mortality with theirs, to see ourselves as little *cosmoi* just as intense and complex as Hamlet, and just as doomed. At its worst, this is self-aggrandizement. In its milder forms, it is part of the universality we ought to expect of tragedy. We make it part of ourselves. To experience a tragic work of art should change our lives. But give us a coherent world outlook it will not.

Tragedy is at least theoretically compatible with any ideology. People have doubted that it can survive a redemptive world outlook, but this is in fact true only of a facile or *post facto* kind of redemption. Brecht can write his Marxist tragedies because the Revolution is so terribly far away, and the world before it is debased. Hochhuth's successful play, *Der Stellvertreter*, shows a man damned by church law for acting consistently in accordance with Christian principles. Traditionally, too, we have the redemptive ending of *Oedipus Coloneus* as a model. There the ending does not negate the suffering, it gives it meaning. For both Brecht and Hochhuth there is suffering on all sides, and no amount of ideology or theology is going to disguise it. These are paradoxes, and tragedy thrives on them. Only an outlook that forbids paradox is incapable of supporting it.

Tragedy has allied with mysticism in Yeats, existentialism in Sartre's *Les Mouches*, Freudianism in *Mourning Becomes Electra*, aesthetic nihilism in *Long Day's Journey into Night*, and naturalism in Dreiser. Flexibility is one of its central and essential norms. It is for this reason that the theorist does best to give as open-ended a description as possible. If tragedy is to be taken as a conflict of orders, it is very hard to restrict what these orders can be. If the tragic hero is to be understood as extreme, there is no way to prescribe what extremity will be his. In many ways, that theory of tragedy is best which specifies least.

Bibliography of Works on Tragedy

Abel, Lionel, ed., *Moderns on Tragedy*, New York, 1967.

Auerbach, Erich, *Mimesis*, Princeton, 1953.

Calarco, N. Joseph, *Tragic Being*, Minneapolis, 1969.

Dodds, E. R., *The Greeks and the Irrational*, Berkeley, 1951.

Domenach, Jean-Marie, *Le Retour du Tragique*, Paris, 1967.

Else, Gerald, *Aristotle's Poetics: The Argument*, Cambridge, Mass., 1957.

————, *The Origin and Early Form of Greek Tragedy*, Cambridge, Mass., 1965.

Fergusson, Francis, *The Idea of a Theatre*, Princeton, 1949.

————, introduction to *Aristotle's Poetics*, S. H. Butcher, trans., New York, 1961.

Finley, John H., Jr., *Four Stages of Greek Thought*, Stanford, 1966.

Frye, Northrop, *The Anatomy of Criticism*, Princeton, 1957.

Grube, G. M. A., ed., *Aristotle on Poetry and Style*, Indianapolis, 1958.

Haigh, A. E., *The Tragic Drama of the Greeks*, Oxford, 1896.

Harrison, Jane, *Themis*, Cambridge, 1912, rev. 1927.

Kaufmann, Walter, *Tragedy and Philosophy*, Garden City, N.Y., 1968.

Kermode, Frank, *The Sense of an Ending*, Oxford, 1967.

Krieger, Murray, *The Tragic Vision*, New York, 1960.

Lucas, F. L., *Tragedy: Serious Drama in Relation to Aristotle's Poetics*, rev. ed., New York, 1962.

Mandel, Oscar, *A Definition of Tragedy*, New York, 1961.

Matthiessen, F. O., *American Renaissance*, New York, 1941.

Michel, Laurence, and Richard B. Sewall, eds., *Tragedy: Modern Essays in Criticism*, Englewood Cliffs, N.J., 1963.

Muller, Herbert J., *The Spirit of Tragedy*, New York, 1956.

Murray, Gilbert, *Five Stages of Greek Religion*, Garden City, 1955.

Myers, Henry Alonzo, *Tragedy: A View of Life*, Ithaca, 1956.

Pickard-Cambridge, A. W., *Dithyramb, Tragedy and Comedy*, Oxford, 1927.

Sewall, Richard B., *The Vision of Tragedy*, New Haven, 1959.

Steiner, George, *The Death of Tragedy*, New York, 1961.

Thomson, George, *Aeschylus and Athens*, New York, 1968.

Unamuno, Miguel de, *Tragic Sense of Life*, J. E. Crawford, trans., New York, 1954.

Williams, Raymond, *Modern Tragedy*, Stanford, 1966.

Index

Nietzsche, Friedrich Wilhelm, *Der Fall Wagner*, 143; *Die Geburt der Tragödie*, 12-23, 57, 59-60, 67-69, 77-78, 98, 108-109, 112-116, 118-120, 125, 142-144, 151-152, 160-163, 166

Olson, Charles, *Call Me Ishmael*, 45
O'Neill, Eugene, *Long Day's Journey into Night*, 98, 171; *Mourning Becomes Electra*, 104, 171
Orestes, 6, 8, 28, 47, 99-100, 130, 136

Peisistratos, 19-20
Pickard-Cambridge, A. W., 13
Pirandello, Luigi, *Così è (se vi pare)*, 131
Pound, Ezra, 106
Proust, Marcel, 155
Pythagoras, 22, 161-163

Racine, Jean, 6, 11, 136
Resnais, Alain, *L'Année dernière à Marienbad*, 131
Rilke, Rainer Maria, 158, 167
Rossetti, Dante Gabriel, 66

Sartre, Jean-Paul, 98; *Les mouches*, 104, 171
Schechner, Richard, *Dionysos in '69*, 132-135
Schiller, Johann Christoph Friedrich von, 11; *Maria Stuart*, 27-28, 32
Schopenhauer, Arthur, 60, 74, 83; *Die Welt als Wille und Vorstellung*, 139-158

Seneca, 9
Shakespeare, William, 5-6, 11, 22-24, 26, 48, 78, 118, 125, 139, 141-142, 153; *Hamlet*, 9-10, 21, 57, 86, 93-95, 164-165, 170; *King Lear*, 10, 42-45, 86, 93-95, 106, 109, 165; *Macbeth*, 10, 29, 38, 45, 62, 165; *Othello*, 10, 45
Shelley, Percy Bysshe, 5; *Prometheus Unbound*, 12, 26
Slatoff, Walter, 111
Socrates, 87, 161, 166
Sophocles, *Ajax*, 165; *Antigone*, 13-15, 160; *Oedipus Coloneus*, 24, 30, 79-81, 142, 171; *Oedipus Rex*, 38, 80-84
Steiner, George, viii
Swinburne, A. C., 65, 84
Synge, John Millington, *Deirdre of the Sorrows*, 66; *The Playboy of the Western World*, 93

Thespis, 8, 114
Thomson, George, 162
Tragedy, Absolutism, 32-39, 49-56, 67, 72, 74-75, 88-89, 139-140, 156
Athenian, 3, 9, 11, 23, 24, 118, 125, 134, 136
Catharsis, 116, 140, 158, 167-168
Chorus, 3, 9-12, 59, 61, 78, 85, 97, 104, 108-116, 117-136
and Christianity, 68, 87, 91, 94, 99, 104-105, 120, 171
and Class, 56-57, 88, 124, 128, 144, 163-164
and Comedy, 146-147, 153

Princeton Essays in Literature

Advisory Committee: Joseph Bauke, Robert Fagles, Claudio Guillén, Robert Maguire

Library of Congress Cataloging in Publication Data

Lenson, David, 1945-
  Achilles' choice.

  (Princeton essays in literature)
  Includes index.
    1. Tragedy.   2. Tragedy—History and criticism.
  3. Drama—History and criticism.   1. Title.
  PN1892.L46   809'.91'6   75-2996
  ISBN 0-691-06292-7